THE
TRANSFORMATIONAL
CONSUMER

Δ

**FUEL A LIFELONG LOVE AFFAIR WITH YOUR CUSTOMERS
BY HELPING THEM GET HEALTHIER, WEALTHIER, AND WISER**

TARA-NICHOLLE
NELSON

BK

Berrett–Koehler Publishers, Inc.
a BK Business book

Berrett-Koehler Publishers, Inc.
1333 Broadway, Suite 1000
Oakland, CA 94612-1921
Tel: (510) 817-2277 Fax: (510) 817-2278 www.bkconnection.com

Ordering Information
Quantity sales. Special discounts are available on quantity purchases by corporations, associations, and others. For details, contact the "Special Sales Department" at the Berrett-Koehler address above.
Individual sales. Berrett-Koehler publications are available through most bookstores. They can also be ordered directly from Berrett-Koehler:
Tel: (800) 929-2929; Fax: (802) 864-7626; www.bkconnection.com
Orders for college textbook/course adoption use. Please contact Berrett-Koehler: Tel: (800) 929-2929; Fax: (802) 864-7626.
Orders by U.S. trade bookstores and wholesalers. Please contact Ingram Publisher Services, Tel: (800) 509-4887; Fax: (800) 838-1149; E-mail: customer.service@ingrampublisherservices.com; or visit www.ingrampublisherservices.com/Ordering for details about electronic ordering.

Berrett-Koehler and the BK logo are registered trademarks of Berrett-Koehler Publishers, Inc.

Printed in the United States of America

Berrett-Koehler books are printed on long-lasting acid-free paper. When it is available, we choose paper that has been manufactured by environmentally responsible processes. These may include using trees grown in sustainable forests, incorporating recycled paper, minimizing chlorine in bleaching, or recycling the energy produced at the paper mill.

Library of Congress Cataloging-in-Publication Data

Names: Nelson, Tara-Nicholle, author.
Title: The transformational consumer : fuel a lifelong love affair with your customers by helping them get healthier, wealthier, and wiser / Tara-Nicholle Nelson.
Description: 1 Edition. | Oakland, CA : Berrett-Koehler Publishers, [2017]
Identifiers: LCCN 2016043949 | ISBN 9781626568839 (hardcover)
Subjects: LCSH: Consumer satisfaction. | Marketing.
Classification: LCC HF5415.335 .N45 2017 | DDC 658.8/343—dc23
LC record available at https://lccn.loc.gov/2016043949

First Edition
21 20 19 18 17 16   10 9 8 7 6 5 4 3 2 1
Cover design by Wes Youssi
Interior illustration by Laurel Muller

This book is dedicated to Channing Dawson, Pete Flint and Sami Inkinen, Michael and Albert Lee, and all the other entrepreneurs who are committed to building thriving businesses while modeling vulnerability and service.

Contents

Thirty Years of Transformation

I've been working on this book since I was nine years old. Allow me to share a little with you about how I got from there to here. My story is the story of a Transformational Consumer. It's also the story of why this book and the Transformational Consumer insights framework at its center both exist.

In my ninth year, my parents owned a racquet club and gym, where I spent a couple of days a week doing step aerobics with a room full of middle-age women, clad (them, not me) in leotards, tights, leg warmers, and high-top Reeboks. I'd watch them cycle in and out, noting which ones showed up all the time and who struggled to keep coming. I listened to them talk about their diets, their clothes, their instructors, even the gym itself with fondness and excitement—especially those who felt like this routine was helping them lose weight.

Even back then, I was fascinated to watch people fall off and hop back on the wagon, to see how they would create little fitness tribes with the people they saw every day at the club. I was mesmerized by the waves of people in and out of this business, which was holding this precious space for their health and, in many respects, their happiness, their energy, and their power to move, live, and be who they wanted to be.

When I was 14, I first read *Quantum Healing*, by Deepak Chopra.[1] I became obsessed with two concepts in the book. The first is that every single cell in our entire bodies is reborn every seven years, giving our bodies an immense capacity for healing. The second is that our mindset and thinking could impact our physical state. This blew my entire mind. I had a number of family members who were ill and dying, at the time, of high blood pressure, heart disease, and diabetes. If this book was right, it seemed, people had great power to change the course of their physical health for the better, if only they could get a handle on their minds and their behavior.

A couple of years later, my life took a little detour, as lives do. I got pregnant, married, and graduated from high school a year early, in that order.

I started college at age 16, had my son during winter break of my freshman year, and went back to class. Through a series of miracles, I got scholarships, graduated, and earned bachelor's and master's degrees in psychology, before moving a few hours north of my hometown to go to law school at UC Berkeley. This move happened the same summer I lost 60 pounds, got certified as a personal trainer, and got out of a bad marriage.

I put myself through law school as a personal trainer. After graduating, I practiced the law for a couple of years, representing people who had been sued civilly and charged criminally for the same conduct. Ultimately, I ended up representing a few bad-apple real estate agents whose disturbingly lackadaisical approach to their clients' transactions, flexible lifestyles, and income (much more than mine) inspired me to make a career change. "I can do this better," I thought.

So I got a real estate broker's license, quit my lawyer job, and hung out my shingle in the field of Bay Area real estate, right around the peak of the market in 2005. I represented a bunch of people just like me: smart, young professionals, buying their first homes. (I'd bought mine right after graduation.) These people researched everything. But they were often very intimidated by the prospect of jumping into the insane market climate of overbidding and over-asking offers.

Sitting with my buyer clients in the car, I spotted a lot of patterns in what people wanted out of their transactions. They didn't want houses. They wanted lifestyle design. They were looking to this single-largest purchase they had ever made to change their lives, careers, businesses, finances, and even their relationships with their kids, partners, and parents, for the better.

But I also watched and wrestled with a handful of my first few home-buyer clients as they made decisions I believed pulled against the direction of their original vision. I asked some agents in my office how I could help manage the emotions and decision traps I saw clients falling into over and over again. Their reply? "Let the market educate your clients." Meaning: let them lose the houses they love, and they'll get beaten down. Then, they'll take your advice.

I rejected this. Using what I knew how to do, I sat down and created a curriculum for home buyers and required every single person or couple who wanted me to show them houses to sit down and go over it with me in the coffee shop or at my office before we ever even got in the car.

The curriculum was essentially a flowchart on which the first event was the initial coffee-shop meeting and the last event was move-in. But then I annotated it heavily, going beyond the standard "how-to," wrapping in "what to expect" and "mindset management."

And things changed, fast. My clients went from making six or seven offers before they'd get a home to making two or three. I even had a client report that she started to freak out at one point, pulled out the chart, remembered that I'd told her she would freak out the night she signed a particular document, and went back to bed.

I turned that flowchart into a seminar, and then I wrote it up into a book, which I self-published. I like to say that I sold ten books, but the tenth was a big sale—to HGTV.

One of the founders of HGTV, a brilliant gent named Channing Dawson, had found my book and called me up asking if the company could license the book as seed content for a digital real estate site it was starting up. Of course, I said yes. And in the same deal, HGTV hired me as a digital-content marketing consultant, with my first project being to break down my 400-page book into hundreds of web articles, several video webisode series (starring me), and PR campaigns.

For the next three years, I had a contract with HGTV, in which I made more money the more traffic I could drive to its website. (This was helpful, as the real estate market was starting to crash, and I needed the income.) The levers I could pull to increase site traffic were few: a spokesperson (me), HGTV's media training, its PR team, and any sort of content I could think to create.

This consulting gig became an intensive real-time adventure in using content marketing to drive digital business results, before the phrase "content marketing" really even existed. I would put together lists of tips, search trends, cities lists, and answers to questions I was hearing a lot from my buyer clients or visitors to the HGTV site. I'd give the tips out on our site and on TV, pitch them to the big Internet portals like AOL and Yahoo!, and place them on blogs and other media outlets.

And we got it down to a science. I'd fly to New York every quarter, get up at three a.m. to do an early-morning satellite media tour, do a couple of spots on morning prime-time shows like *Good Morning America*, and then go pitch magazine editors to feature our content. We built relationships with producers and editors, who were thrilled with my fancy credentials and what they called my yoga-teacher demeanor. Viewers wrote in to us, telling us how much better they felt when I'd been on the air, even though I didn't always have the best news to give about the tumbling real estate market.

Every time I went on TV, the site hit record traffic.

Spotting patterns in what people wanted in their lives and their obstacles, then serving them how-to, what-to-expect, and mindset-management content just plain worked.

Soon, I was offered an in-house marketing role at Trulia.com, a real estate search engine and competitor of HGTV's site, managing consumer content, marketing, and PR and serving as the company's spokesperson. We developed a whole program out of engaging users on the company's products with content, helping them save, invest, spend less, and make wise real estate decisions. We created recurring PR campaigns featuring the company's data and spokespeople that routinely earned coverage in hundreds of media outlets and brought over 11 million people to the most trafficked single-author real estate blog ever.

I left Trulia to work at a boutique tech PR agency in San Francisco, as the VP of digital and content. I launched brand-new products *outside* of real estate with these strategies. And they still worked. They worked in mobile security. They worked in cosmetics. They worked on all kinds of apps. They worked with digital textbooks. They worked when I was the spokesperson and when I wasn't. I left the agency to start my own company doing the same work, but I wanted to focus on companies that were doing work that would change people's lives for the better. And I had the best clients ever. ModCloth. Eventbrite. I continued to work with Trulia, but as my client instead of as my employer.

And then one day I got a call from MyFitnessPal, the world's largest fitness app. The company was then eight years old and had 45 million users. After working with the company as a consultant, I ended up staying on as its first and only VP of marketing.

Over the next 18 months, I built a marketing team that would use customer research, digital marketing, and content to help the company double to over 100 million customers and increase customer engagement by 22%. We went from raising an $18 million Series A investment round when I first arrived to selling the company to Under Armour for $475 million, in less than two years.

In an age when disengagement was rampant and many people were saying that email is dead, here are a few Tweets we received in the early days of the MyFitnessPal content program:

▲ "Whoever does the newsletter at @MyFitnessPal, you're awesome. 🧖 #fitnessmotivation"

▲ "@MyFitnessPal Just wanted to say how much I love your blog. Every article is relevant to me and an interesting read. Very well done."

▲ "@MyFitnessPal love your newsletters very interesting articles . . . keep them coming! :D"

This was not an isolated occurrence. I used to keep a massive file of the exact same sorts of notes while I was working on the content programming at Trulia. One I remember by heart. It was an email that started out, verbatim, "Your newsletter just saved my marriage." Now, I can't tell you what was going on in that marriage. But I can tell you that it was clear the content was connecting with people and their real issues, their real journeys. They cared about it enough to open it, click on it, read it, and rave about it.

What I've seen, time after time, is that billions of people worldwide are coming to the marketplace specifically looking for the products and services and brands that can help them live healthier, wealthier, and wiser lives. I've seen that they become deeply devoted, repeat customers of the companies that help them do this more effectively, easily, beautifully, or joyously than they could do it on their own.

After a decade of spotting these patterns and helping companies create thriving businesses from this point of view, I created a new consumer insights framework for helping companies spot opportunities for innovation, drive customer loyalty, and build beloved brands and content that people care about. I started to speak and write about my firsthand observations that the companies that grow and win in this era of social media and content marketing are not the companies that focus on boomers, moms, or millennials. They are the companies that focus on serving a massive, rapidly growing customer segment I call Transformational Consumers and unlocking progress along their journeys to live healthier, wealthier, and wiser lives.

If you're looking for the lever to pull to get your company growing, winning, and out of the tired old story of disengaged customers and employees, you are in the right place. Serving the Transformational Consumer is that lever. But it doesn't *just* help you escape that old narrative. It also unlocks the possibility for a transcendent new story: the story of a wild, lifelong love affair with your customers.

How to Transcend the Transactional

Advertisements are so numerous that they are very negligently perused, and it is therefore become necessary to gain attention by magnificence of promises and by eloquence sometimes sublime and sometimes pathetic.

—SAMUEL JOHNSON, 1759

Have you ever started up your car and had the warning bell start going off, but it wasn't obvious what was making it ring? You open and shut the doors, check to make sure everyone's seat belts are on, slam the trunk a couple of times, and still it dings. Only after you give up and realize you're driving against resistance do you realize that your parking brake is on. Unclick it, and you're *off*.

That's what I see happening with entrepreneurs and executives in every size of business, in every sector, around the world.

I talk with these people every day for a living. There are three things they say they're most stressed about:

1. Growing the business (Growth)
2. Beating the competition (Winning)
3. Posting the right "content" to the right social media channel at the right time (Content)

While the first two of these are worthy objectives, the levers that most executives and entrepreneurs try to pull in order to achieve them are, like slamming the trunk, barking up the wrong tree. The number-one limiting factor of almost every business is neither growth nor the competition. It is disengagement. It has been since at least 1759. More on that in just a bit.

The third question is a beast of its own. "What should we do on social media?" sucks up a stunningly disproportionate amount of time and energy at the highest levels of almost every company I meet for such a tactical issue.

1

These are the wrong questions. We're having the wrong conversations. Here's how I know.

I was the VP of marketing for the world's largest digital health company. The company was called MyFitnessPal. Our logo was a little orange dancer. We called her "tiny dancer." She was clip art, from a time when the founder built the app in a back room, just he and his cat.

Yet, with these brand assets, the founder grew that company to have 45 million users, over eight years. Then we grew from 45 million to over 100 million users in 18 months. We started a blog with zero readers that had ten million uniques a month less than ten months later.

And we did it with zero paid advertising.

How?

We paid attention to the humanity of the people we served. We paid attention to how they wanted their lives to be different and how we could help them achieve that. This deep, human motivation—transformation—is one of the most elemental reasons people do the things they do. The drive for their lives to be different and better than they are right now is the pure, primal force underlying nearly every purchase decision and brand interaction people make.

In particular, there are three ways in which people have wanted their lives to be different throughout human history. And each of these involves a set of behavior changes that are extraordinarily difficult for people to make.

▲ They want to be healthier.

▲ They want to be wealthier.

▲ They want to be wiser.

Those of us who have taken on business as our life's work must now elevate our thinking. We must dare to be different. Let's stop fixating on which pic to post on which channel. Instead, dedicate yourself and your company to the endeavor of becoming an agent and facilitator of the transformations that people want to make in their lives.

That's what we did at MyFitnessPal. Our business model, our product, our marketing, even our internal culture—everything about the company was devoted to helping our customers change their behavior to make progress on their transformational journeys.

That's how we achieved greatness. Even with an orange dancer logo. Even with the word "pal" in our brand name.

This might sound like it's difficult to do if your company sells soap or paper products. It might sound impossible if your company has sold drugs or home-improvement supplies for 100 years. This might sound really hard if your business model is B2B enterprise software or retail or grocery or even apparel.

Trust me when I say that it can be done. And if you choose to take on this challenge, which this book explains how to do, you can opt out of the disengagement epidemic and transcend the transactional nature of your company's relationships with customers.

Meet the Protagonist of Your New Love Story: The Transformational Consumer

Transformational Consumers are a massive and growing group of people who see life as a never-ending series of projects to live healthier, wealthier, wiser lives.

They spend a great deal of their time and money on the products, services, and content that can help them make these changes.

They are early adopters. They influence the buying behavior of everyone around them. And they engage in joyful, two-way love affairs with the brands that change their lives.

They are triathletes, Crossfitters, and fitness walkers. They do Soul-Cycle and the senior exercise classes at Kaiser Permanente. Some of them are hardcore health nuts. Others might call their lifestyles "healthy-ish."

If you have been vegan *and* Paleo, at different times in your life, you might be a Transformational Consumer.

Transformational Consumers pick carefully the things they put in, on, and around their bodies.

They are always studying a course in something, exploring a new certification, or starting a business on the side. They read lots of business and wisdom literature, such as this book.

They experiment with frugality. They think a lot about designing their lives and course correcting the total picture of what they do with their work, their careers, and their time. They may have rejected a regular day job to drive for Uber or rent out their spare space on Airbnb, so they can work on their art or their entrepreneurial endeavors.

The specific aspirations of an individual Transformational Consumer at a given time don't matter right now. For now, the most important thing to understand is how these people define and view themselves. Transformational Consumers consciously view themselves as committed to growth, development, change for the better, and constantly making progress toward living a healthier, wealthier, wiser life.

And Transformers are the companies that transcend the transactional by understanding, reaching, engaging, and serving Transformational Consumers in the same way these people see themselves: through the lens of change.

Disengaged and Disgusted: The Trouble with Transactional

Most companies are very fixated on growing sales and increasing revenue. So they look at customers through the lens of the transaction, tasking their teams with one overall objective: how can we get people to buy more of what we sell? Even so-called Customer Relationship Management and loyalty programs often focus most closely on the desired transactions themselves, funneling customers toward making purchases and rewarding them when they do.

This transactional focus pervades the relationships these companies have with their customers. Strictly transactional relationships with your customers are a quid pro quo. You provide a thing, and they buy the thing. That's that.

The thing is, this type of tit-for-tat, transactional relationship is what my dear grandmother would call a hard row to hoe. Because it's a row that has to be constantly seeded. Incessantly seeded. Expensively seeded.

And that's exactly what most companies do. They hire growth hackers. They pay for "user acquisition." They spend millions on brand marketing. They spend all their money trying to plant new seeds in new fields, getting new customers into the top of their funnel, because they can't count on their existing customers to visit again, buy more, or get their friends to come into the fold. This is a losing game, unless you can count on it being cheaper to acquire new users over the long run than to engage the customers you already have.

Spending millions to acquire disengaged "customers" who buy your product or download your app and never buy it again, never tell anyone about it, never read or watch your marketing messages again is an unsustainable business model.

On the other hand, any company, of any size, in any sector will be successful if it engages two audiences, over and over again: customers and employees.

Unfortunately, most companies are not doing so well with either:

▲ One in four mobile app users abandon apps after a single use.[1]

▲ Viewers avoid well over 60% of commercial messages simply by turning their heads.[2]

▲ Nearly 70% of employees, the people we *pay* to be engaged, rank somewhere between mildly disinterested and actively, toxically hateful when it comes to their employer and their work.[3]

Let that sink in for a minute. *We can't even pay people to be engaged.*

The other problem with taking the transactional approach is that it tempts companies into short-term thinking and bad behavior. Imagine, if you will, that a *New York Times* article about your company triggered readers to describe your company as "cravenly amoral," your products as a "dystopian disaster," and your strategy as "crony capitalism." That'd be a nightmare, right?

Well, that nightmare came true for a number of Big Food companies in February 2013, when an excerpt from Michael Moss's Big Food exposé *Salt, Sugar, Fat: How the Food Giants Hooked Us* ran in the *New York Times*, eliciting those real-life reader quotes.[4] Under the headline "The Extraordinary Science of Addictive Junk Food," the piece told how Moss discovered overwhelming evidence that food companies make "a conscious effort to get people hooked on foods that are convenient and inexpensive."[5]

Unfortunately, these same foods played a disproportionate role in kickstarting America's obesity and diabetes epidemics.

Moss wrote of meeting a pioneering "food optimizer" who had "no qualms about his own pioneering work on discovering what industry insiders now regularly refer to as 'the bliss point' or any of the other systems that helped food companies create the greatest amount of crave." He wrote about a meeting he had with the food scientist Steven Witherly, bringing the well-known food optimizer a bag of junk food from which Witherly immediately extracted Cheetos:

> "This," Witherly said, "is one of the most marvelously constructed foods on the planet, in terms of pure pleasure." He ticked off a dozen attributes of the Cheetos that make the brain say more. But the one he focused on most was the puff's uncanny ability to melt in the mouth. "It's called vanishing caloric density," Witherly said. "If something melts down quickly, your brain thinks that there's no calories in it . . . you can just keep eating it forever."[6]

The result? More Cheetos sold. More transactions. In the short term.

This decades-long campaign to get people addicted to unhealthful foods is exactly what people think of when they think of companies trying to create habit-forming products. They think of big, evil conglomerates on a sinister mission to get people addicted to retail, screens, friend feeds, and bad foods, while they laugh all the way to the bank.

This sort of bad behavior happens when a sector of companies has exclusively transactional relationships with customers.

Cravenly amoral. Disgust, distrust, and, ultimately, disengagement. (*Fortune* reports that soda sales are down in 2016 for the 11th year running.)[7] That taking a transactional approach to your customers is bad for business seems like a serious understatement.

What Does a Love Affair with Transformational Consumers Look Like?

This whole behavior-changing business scenario *could* have played out a totally different way. It's already starting to, in some of the great businesses of our time. The flip-side conclusion of Moss's investigation is that businesses *are* in the position to understand how to change and influence people's behavior, even the hardest ones to change. There's nothing that says companies can't wield that influence for good, instead of for evil.

From this vantage point, the Transformational Consumer framework poses a challenge, a revolutionary new possibility: what if companies used what we know about building habits and changing behavior to help people create the healthy, prosperity-inducing habits that people are out there trying to build on their own? What if we aligned our business models with people's personal goals for themselves, to change their behavior for the healthier, wealthier, and wiser?

Massive, massive change, that's what would happen. Healthy, prosperous people whose behavior aligns with their higher hopes and dreams for their lives.

And the consumer response to businesses would change, too. Love and long-term, sustainable profitability. That would happen, too.

These "what ifs" point to an alternative realm of possibility for company-customer relationships, a path beyond the epidemics of distrust and disengagement. In this new realm, business becomes a force for beneficial transformation in individual customers' lives. There, companies and their customers have real, deep, lasting connections. Customers look forward excitedly to the opportunity to buy their products, tell their friends about it, open, click, like, and review.

I've seen it happen, firsthand. I saw it when I worked with HGTV, when I worked at Trulia, and definitely as the chief marketer for MyFitnessPal. This new possibility for business is anxiously waiting in the wings, just itching to replace the tired status quo of companies begging for attention, stuck and limited by disgust and disengagement.

In this new realm, customers are the hero of their own life journey. They take on a never-ending series of quests to change their lives for the better, coming back from each quest challenged and changed. Every time they go out on a quest to live a healthier, wealthier, wiser life, they seek and find mentors, advisers, and tools to help them overcome their challenges.

And every time they return home from a quest, they inspire their friends and loved ones to go out on life-changing quests of their own—to be the heroes of their own journeys.

In this new realm, these thriving, engaging companies have a single thing in common: they *are* the knowledgeable mentor, the compassionate adviser, and the invaluable, transformational tools these customers can't bear to be without (and can't stop telling their friends and loved ones about, either).

This new future is already reality for start-ups like the ones I mentioned earlier. It is also the new reality for much-larger, more mature incumbent, nondigital companies, such as CVS/health and Target. It is possible for companies in the health, fitness, and lifestyle-design industries, but it is also already manifesting itself for companies in much less obvious verticals, such as Airbnb and Apple.

There is a uniquely human force that these brands have all tapped into, whether by design or out of their sheer love for their users. This force is bigger than any brand, bigger than any product, bigger even than any demographic group—even millennials, even boomers, even moms.

This future, in which companies engage in wild, two-way love affairs with their customers by helping them along their journeys, is available to any company or brand that gets serious about tapping into this force.

It is available to you and your company.

This force is the human drive for transformation.

And the companies that are tapping into this force have pioneered a path to the other end of the engagement spectrum, with their customers and employees.

They are consistently ranked as the most innovative companies in the world.

They are consistently ranked among the most beloved, engaging brands.

They consistently achieve stellar growth and beat their competition.

They are consistently crowned the best places to work.

By helping their target audience make the critical life changes they crave, these companies have become linchpins in the lives of a powerful group of consumers. They have engineered—and sometimes reengineered— everything about their business to serve Transformational Consumers.

And Transformational Consumers are responding. They engage in love affairs with the companies that help them change their lives, their habits, their bodies, and their finances for the better all the time. But these love affairs don't always look the way you might expect. Brand-love, affinity, or sentiment metrics begin to capture the emotion of this phenomenon, but they do little to reveal the profound business impact of the "love" of a Transformational Consumer.

Some of those love affairs are wild and rollicking and sexy. The love of some Transformational Consumers for lululemon gear or SoulCycle spin classes is something they proudly proclaim, literally wearing their hearts on their sleeves (and headbands and pant legs). This doesn't mean these relationships are necessarily short-term infatuations. Rather, the branding and subject matter and life-improving impact of these brands has enough power and cachet that people tend to talk about them, a lot.

But many Transformational Consumer love affairs with the products that make their lives healthier, wealthier, and wiser look much more like a long, lovely, devoted marriage than a heady entanglement. Customers may not wander about starry-eyed or head over heels, but they do read the blog every day. They do open the newsletters. They do share the content. They do buy or use the product every day, week, month, or every time it becomes relevant in their lives. They do tell their friends, when asked, what their go-to budget or online learning software is and who their go-to real estate broker, life coach, CPA, or insurance agent is.

I may not go about wearing T-shirts proclaiming my love for my go-to protein powder, but I buy it every month.

Unprecedented growth, beating the competition, lifelong customer loyalty, and word-of-mouth referrals: that's what it looks like when Transformational Consumers engage in lifelong love affairs with the companies that help them change their lives.

How to Use This Framework

Leaders, brands, and companies use the Transformational Consumer framework to get clear direction and answers to the kinds of questions that executive teams struggle with regularly:

▲ What products should we build or invest in next?

▲ Will this marketing, message, content, or campaign resonate with people? What messages will work?

▲ What features do our customers really want—and will they want next year or three years from now?

▲ How should we take this product to market? How should we package and market it?

▲ Where are our customers, and what do they care about?

▲ Why are our customers disengaged, and what should we do about it?

It provides direction on some of the big, strategic questions to ask and clear direction for how to answer them:

▲ What is the human-scale problem we aim to solve, as a company?

▲ What do we have to do over and over in order to achieve the impact we want to have on the world?

▲ Should we focus on growth, engagement, or both, and which teams should be held to account for these objectives?

▲ How might we drive innovation here, on an ongoing basis?

And it also translates into more tactical guidance for R&D, product launches, and marketing campaigns:

▲ How can we reach our audiences? Who are they, where are they, and what messages will resonate with them?

▲ How can we create lifelong relationships with customers?

How to Use This Book

First, I'll introduce you to the Transformational Consumer in a lot more depth. I'll help you to understand exactly why it's so important that you continue to study, reach, and engage these people. The business case for behavior change is a compelling one.

Then I'll issue a call to action, a call to adventure, really, to you as a business leader.

The last half of the book is the change-management section. That's where you'll learn how to embark on the journey of actually reorienting your company to transcend the transactional by focusing on serving the Transformational Consumer. I will walk you through the process of elevating the way your teams think about five elemental focus points of your business: your customer, what you sell, your marketing, your competition, and your team.

All along the way, I'll share stories, case studies, insightful data, and tools for asking higher-level questions and getting transformative answers.

Painlessly Get This Book into Your Brain

When I embarked on this project, I was told that people would *buy* this book, but 95% of them likely wouldn't read it. I reject that. So I took it as a content strategy challenge.

I've built some recurring features that you'll find throughout the book with the intention of boosting the chances that the most important content will have the opportunity to impact your business, your life, your team, and the lives of your customers and your employees, for the better:

▲ **Transformational Takeaways.** I've put the three most important points, in one-liner format, near the beginning of every chapter instead of at the end, so you know from the start where it fits into what's important to you.

▲ **Digital Dossier.** If you're more of a video person, have a short attention span for the written word, or simply want to continue your own journey, the interactive materials in the Digital Dossier at TransformationalConsumer.com is for you. There, you'll also find a set of free resources to help you gear up, craft, and carry out your individual and organizational action plans for transcending the transactional.

▲ **Stories.** Neuroscience researchers have found that our brains light up for several days when we read or hear a story. My mission is to help you meet, understand, reach, and engage the Transformational Consumer primarily by telling you stories and sharing case studies that make the case and teach the frameworks. Some will be from brands that are clearly transformational, some will not. But all will help illustrate the frameworks and flesh them out in a way your brain can retain.

▲ **Transformer case studies.** These case studies showcase examples of strategic product, business model, marketing, and cultural moves that a series of world-class companies have made to connect with Transformational Consumers. They then explain how these moves played out.

▲ **The Transformational Consumer Self-Assessment: What Do You Need to Rethink First?** To help you convert the concepts and marching orders in this book into an individualized personal and organizational roadmap, I've created the Transformational Consumer Self-Assessment: What Do You Need to Rethink First? (available from Berrett-Koehler Publishers at www.bkconnection .com/transformationalconsumer-sa). Take the assessment either right before or after you read chapters 5 through 9, to start sequencing your action plan and transcending the transactional.

If I tried to walk you step by step through how to execute every conceivable tactic for engaging the Transformational Consumer, this book would be many volumes long. Worse, it would be out of date by the time it went to press. This is not a textbook, though I do provide frameworks, principles, and guideposts for taking action on these insights.

My mission for this book is to impact the lives of billions of *your* customers for the better, by driving a fundamental change in the way you understand, serve, and connect with them. I want to change what you're thinking about as you lead or run your business, whether you're a personal trainer or the CEO of a public company. I want to change how you think about your customers. I want to elevate the conversation.

And I want to do that by injecting it with the beautiful vision for the world of customer-company relationships that I know, from firsthand experience, is possible. I want to share what I know works to help companies transcend the fray and engage customers in wild, two-way love affairs, even in this era of digital overwhelm and customer fatigue.

Disengagement is not a digital problem. It is a human problem. And the solution is human, too. Once you understand the powerful motivation of the human drive to live healthier, wealthier, and wiser, clarity will replace confusion about how to connect with people.

Eternal principles of story and content and humanity and transformation will replace the dramatics about what social media channel you *simply must* be active on (this week). Deep insight into your customers' journeys will provide clear, self-updating direction on where and how to reach them at any given time.

Every team and initiative of your business will be able to operate in a way that drives change for Transformational Consumers.

This is how your company becomes great: by transcending the transactional. And how you transcend the transactional is by becoming a force for transformation in the lives of the people you serve.

CHAPTER ONE

Meet the Transformational Consumer

You see, technically, chemistry is the study of matter, but I prefer to see it as the study of change: Electrons change their energy levels. Molecules change their bonds. Elements combine and change into compounds. But that's all of life, right? It's the constant, it's the cycle. It's solution, dissolution. Just over and over and over. It is growth, then decay, then transformation. It's fascinating really. It's a shame so many of us never take time to consider its implications.

—WALTER WHITE, *BREAKING BAD*, SEASON 1, EPISODE 1

TRANSFORMATIONAL TAKEAWAYS

1. The Personal Disruption Conundrum is the number-one limiting factor of Transformational Consumers.
2. Transformational Consumers are HUMAN.
3. Any product is transformational if people buy it with the motivation of living a healthier, wealthier, and wiser life.

A friend of mine goes by the name of Coach Stevo. Stevo is a sports psychologist and an expert in habit formation. But he got his start as a regular old personal trainer. In fact, in the very earliest days of his career, he was a trainer with a serious niche: people preparing to take the Marine Corps physical exam. He himself had gone from fat to fit in preparation for the Marine physical, and he wanted to pass on what he'd learned. The way he tells it, he would give these cadet hopefuls a program to follow and tell them what to do, and they'd do it.

Done and done.

And then one day, into Stevo's gym walked a woman we'll call Sister Mary Catherine, a retired Irish Catholic nun. It would be foolhardy to let Sister Mary Catherine's soft middle distract you from what would turn out to be her razor-sharp tongue. But Stevo was up for the challenge—he started telling her what to do, giving her exercises and a workout plan to follow, but things didn't quite go as predictably as they had with his uber-motivated clients in the past. She struggled to make progress.

At one point, Sister Mary Catherine called out a big problem she'd seen, something she felt posed the danger of setting her relationship with Stevo up for failure.

She decided to clear things up for her intrepid trainer. "I know what to do," she declared. "I need you to help me make myself do it."

Sister Mary Catherine was what you might call a character. And like all characters, she presented at least one of the elemental characteristics that make up the archetype (that archetype being "Transformational Consumer"). Once we understand an archetype, engaging with the individual characters that spring out of the archetype is a much more vivid, much richer, more real experience. Understand "gangster," and "Don Corleone" is a different, more nuanced being.

Sister Mary Catherine's comment—"I can't make myself do the things I want or need to do"—is the essence of what I call the Personal Disruption Conundrum. The Personal Disruption Conundrum is the number-one limiting factor of people who invest a great deal of their time and money into projects to get healthier, wealthier, or wiser: Transformational Consumers.

Let's explore the core characteristics of the archetype: Transformational Consumers' minds, beliefs, and consumer patterns. This is the first step to engaging with the real Transformational Consumers, the real people, the real characters in your customer base or audience. It's also the first step to helping them take this limit off themselves—and unlimiting your business in the process.

The Defining Characteristics of a Transformational Consumer

Transformational Consumers are the citizens of the world and the web who view life as a continual series of personal disruption campaigns: behavior-change projects to live healthier, wealthier, wiser lives.

They gladly, excitedly invest their time and money on the products, services, and content that can help them solve the Personal Disruption Conundrum.

They are early adopters of new products and technologies that they believe might be able to further their transformational aspirations. They are also highly influential: they influence the buying behavior of everyone around them.

Transformational Consumers engage in joyful, two-way love affairs with the brands that change their lives: using them over and over again, devouring their content, and telling everyone they know about the brands and products that have transformed their lives.

There are five core characteristics of Transformational Consumers. I find them easier to remember with the acronym HUMAN.

H—Focus on joyful prosperity: *healthier*, wealthier, and wiser

U—See life as an *unending* series of personal disruption campaigns

M—Have an extreme growth (versus fixed) *mindset*

A—Have innate or learned bias toward *action*

N—Engage in a *never-ending* search to find products, services, and content that support their behavior-change goals

I have worked from this list of characteristics for years, just on the basis of my own observations and insights doing the work of engaging Transformational Consumers. But as I was working on this book, my company, Transformational Consumer Insights (TCI), partnered with the research technology platform Qualtrics to survey 2,000 U.S. consumers. The objective? To quantify how mainstream this Transformational Consumer phenomenon has become since those days at my parents' racquet club.

The answer we found was undeniable: *very mainstream*. In this survey, the Inaugural Transformational Consumer Insights Study,[1] a full 50% of respondents said they use digital or real-world products *at least several times a week* in an effort to achieve any of a number of health, financial, career, or personal-development aims.

I repeat for emphasis: 50% of U.S. consumers are Transformational Consumers. *This is not a niche.*

Keep in mind, as we learn more about these people, that the last characteristic—consumers' never-ending hunt for products and services and content that support their transformational aspirations—is the single thing that qualifies people as Transformational Consumers.

This tells us *what* these people do, in terms of their consumer behavior.

So what are the other four characteristics? They help flesh out the framework in a critical way. They add meaningful, human insight that explains *why* these people do the things they do, why their consumer behavior is so influenced by their desire to make these core life changes. These instinctive insights were validated when the data showed that people who qualified as Transformational Consumers were more likely to possess all of the other four characteristics than non-Transformational Consumers were, to a statistically significant degree.

Now, let's take the characteristics, one by one.

H—Focus on Joyful Prosperity: *Healthier,* Wealthier, and Wiser

The content, the *substance,* of Transformational Consumers' aspirations that power their consumer behavior is that they simply want to be healthier, wealthier, and wiser. They want to live healthier, wealthier, wiser lives.

I call this desire the pursuit of joyful prosperity. From now on, we'll call healthy, wealthy, and wise, collectively, the Aspirations, with a capital *A,* or refer to them as HWW.[2]

In our seminal Transformational Consumer study, we listed a dozen common goals that people set around their HWW Aspirations. We then asked respondents to identify any of these goals that they were currently taking any action—anything—to pursue.

Transformational Consumers overindexed on every single goal, meaning they were more likely than the average to be working on every one of the health, wealth, or wisdom goals specified. *When compared against non-Transformational Consumers, Transformational Consumers were anywhere from two to four times as likely to be working on a given HWW goal* (see table 1).

Table 1 Comparing the Percentage of Transformational, non-Transformational, and Overall Consumers Actively Trying to Reach Various Goals

Q: I am currently doing something to try to reach the following goals:

	Respondents overall (%)	Transformational Consumers (%)	Non-Transformational Consumers (%)
Eat better	54	63	45
Exercise more	44	56	33
Lose weight	40	47	34
Do more yoga	10	16	5
Save more money	50	61	39
Invest my money more wisely	21	32	10
Earn more money	41	54	27
Hit a retirement target	10	14	6

continued on next page

Table 1 *(continued)*

Q: I am currently doing something to try to reach the following goals:

	Respondents overall (%)	Transformational Consumers (%)	Non-Transformational Consumers (%)
Start a business	8	12	4
Change my career	8	12	5
Earn a certificate, license, or degree	11	17	4
Learn a new skill	23	35	11
Take up a new hobby	20	28	11
Travel more	27	35	18
Be a better parent	17	24	10
Fulfill more of my potential at work	12	20	4
Be a better citizen of the world	22	30	14

Here's a point you'll hear me make over and over: it does not matter how you or I might define which life experiences and subject matters fall within or outside the boundaries of healthy, wealthy, or wise.

What matters is how the Transformational Consumers view, experience, or define healthy, wealthy, and wise.

And they experience them *broadly.* Table 2 depicts just some of the areas of life (and spending) that Transformational Consumers often group within each of the three Aspirations. (Note the overlap. Humans and the way we think about our lives are simply not cut and dry.)

Wise, in particular, can be a little nebulous. It includes anything Transformational Consumers might do in the effort to become a better person, to become self-actualized, or to fulfill their potential in the world.

Transformational Consumers experience the Aspirations as similar, related, and overlapping, in a few different ways.

The first common thread running through the Aspirations is this: that healthy, wealthy, and wise are universally viewed as necessary cornerstones of the good life. You can debate how each of them is defined, but no

Table 2 How Transformational Consumers Experience Healthy, Wealthy, and Wise: Broadly

Healthy	Wealthy	Wise
Health care	Personal finance, savings, and investing	Self-actualization
Pharmaceuticals	B2B and enterprise software	Meditation
Food and eating	Productivity	Lifelong learning and hobbies / skill building
Physical health and fitness	Debt management	Travel
Emotional health	Career development and continuing education	Faith and spirituality
Weight management	Entrepreneurship	Charitable giving
Disease prevention	Real estate and mortgage	Higher education
Sleep	Collaborative consumption (e.g., Airbnb, Lyft, Uber, etc.)	Skill building
Mental health and stress management	Lifestyle design	Emotional health
Wellness	Higher education / open education	Time management and productivity
Holistic health and beauty	Professional development	Organization
Home care and cleaning	Home improvement	Personal growth and development

one really argues that some level of physical and emotional wellness, some level of material provision for needs, and some level of personal development or self-actualization are components of a life well lived.

Transformational Consumers almost always orient their thoughts and actions on each HWW goal in one of three different ways:

▲ They crave to fix, or heal, dysfunction.

▲ They seek to maintain what is functional.

▲ They aim to optimize functioning.

Healing dysfunction. When Transformational Consumers set goals and orient a given Aspiration around fixing dysfunction, they want to come from a state of dysfunction to a state of basic functionality: healing what's unhealthy, fixing what's broken, freeing themselves from the constraints and limitations that result from malfunctions. They tend to think about these objectives as freedom from the friction, pain, or limitation resulting from the malfunction. They just want to be "normal" or "healthy"—the latter term being one they use for solid functioning without impairment in any Aspiration, not just for health.

Common Transformational Consumer goals oriented around fixing dysfunction include the following:

▲ Losing weight

▲ Getting out of debt

▲ Getting out of physical pain

▲ No longer being depressed or anxious

▲ Quitting a terrible day job or "firing" a horrible boss

Maintaining a baseline. On some goals and Aspirations, Transformational Consumer might simply want to maintain a state of healthy, baseline functionality.

Maintaining a healthy baseline is a common motivating factor for the repeat HWW purchases of the Transformational Consumer. *Most of the transformational spending people will do in their lifetime will go toward buying supplies that help them maintain baselines*, trying to make better choices as they carry out various routines:

▲ Cleaning house (Healthy)

▲ Feeding themselves and their children (Healthy)

▲ Preventive health—fitness and wellness, early detection, health maintenance (Healthy)

▲ Saving and investing (Wealthy)

▲ Continuing career education (Wealthy)

▲ Home maintenance and improvement (Wealthy)

▲ Attending worship services (Wise)

▲ Meditation, yoga, and other regular stress-management practices (Healthy/Wise)

▲ Hobbies, workshops, and classes they see as cultivating personal development (Healthy/Wise).

Optimization. The third way Transformational Consumers orient their goals and Aspirations is by aiming to achieve extraordinary performance in one or more areas of their lives.

In, On, and Around

Transformational Consumers spend a lot of time thinking about the healthfulness of the products they put in, on, and around their bodies (and their kids' and pets' bodies, too). This means food and food containers, drugs and pharmacy supplies, bath and body products, feminine hygiene, household cleaners. Even products like diapers, pet food, clothing, and eyewear get extra scrutiny from this consumer group!

"I usually read labels before buying cleaning products."

Non-Transformational Consumers	44%
Transformational Consumers	71%

Transformational Consumers are looking for whole and unprocessed foods, natural cleaners, food-grade bath and body products, and nontoxic mattresses, home furnishings, car seats, and kids' products. The theory is that all of these categories end up making their way into their bodies and ultimately impact their health, for better and for worse.

The life of a Transformational Consumer is a vision quest, powered by optimism and belief in possibilities that many of them have seen only in the lives of people they look up to or in their own minds' eyes. A stunning 82% of Transformational Consumers believe they can get healthier, even as they age, something only 58% of non-Transformational Consumers said they believed.

This visionary optimism and belief among Transformational Consumers that they can live an optimized life is a fundamental, powerful motivator for them. This "optimization" orientation shows up in the form of goals such as the following:

▲ Start a business

▲ Work at the job of my dreams

▲ Be a superfit marathoner/cyclist/yogi/dancer

▲ Have financial freedom

▲ Be able to travel the world and do the work I want

▲ Live a long life

▲ Feel and function better, physically, the older I get

▲ Max out my potential, mastering my professional field or area of expertise

▲ Write a book

"I have a vision for what I want my life to be like."
Non-Transformational Consumers 62%
Transformational Consumers 87%

These optimization-oriented goals are less common than the other orientations. But they are powerful differentiators between Transformational and non-Transformational Consumers. They also surface innovation opportunities for higher-priced business products that Transformational Consumers will view as a deep investment in their future, such as B2B and enterprise software, eCourses, and certification programs.

Twice as many Transformational Consumers surveyed (54%) are actively working to level up their income and earn more money than non-Transformational Consumers (27%). More than three times as many are working on learning a new skill (35% of Transformational vs. 11% of non-Transformational). And over four times as many Transformational Consumers (17%) are currently working toward the goal of earning a certificate, license, or degree as non-Transformational Consumers (4%).

Remember, our job is to think about the Aspirations of the Transformational Consumer the same way they do: broadly and with bold, visionary optimism about what's possible.

Blame it on the dopamine. The second common thread among the Aspirations is this: it's hard to make good habits and hard to break bad habits in the same way, across all of the Aspirations. I blame this on two things: Resistance, which we'll cover in chapter 2, and the neurotransmitter dopamine.

When stimulated by dopamine release, our brains' reward centers shower down an intense, delicious rush of addiction-forming pleasure. We are wired to go to great lengths to trigger this pleasure. This pleasure shows up in multiple forms, including the rush of orgasm, the high of cocaine, and the emotional release of opiates.

The same exact brain centers activate, sending out that same flood of pleasure, when we do things that are considered bad HWW habits. That's where we feel the "comfort" of binging on salty, sugary, and fattily delectable food. It's where we get the hit of gratification from overspending (hence the term "retail therapy"). It's where the alcoholic's relaxed buzz comes from and also where we experience the sweetly numb, hard-to-break mental haze of staring at the screen of our television, laptop, or Facebook feed.

So dopamine fuels and feeds our bad habits across the aspirations. And people find dopamine very, very difficult to overrule across the Aspirations, which one must do in order to build good HWW habits, such as sticking to a budget or eating your vegetables.

U—See Life as an *Unending* Series of Personal Disruption Campaigns

This characteristic has two important parts: (1) the worldview of life as a constant, rolling, overlapping series of projects, and (2) the personally disruptive nature of these projects.

To Transformational Consumers, everything about life is always on the table, always subject to change. They almost always have some sort of life-improvement campaign under way, whether small scale or sweeping.

Seventy-eight percent of Transformational Consumers said they "set goals all the time," compared with 41% of non-Transformational Consumers. And 82% of Transformational Consumers said they feel it's important to reach their full potential before they die. (Contrast this with only 54% of non-Transformational Consumers.)

In fact, it is very common for Transformational Consumers to carry out multiple behavior-change campaigns in their lives simultaneously. In our survey, 90% of Transformational Consumers said that they were in the process of working on at least two health, financial, or personal-development goals, compared with 62% of non-Transformational Consumers. Eighty-two percent of Transformational Consumers were working on three or more goals (vs. 47% of non-Transformational Consumers), and a whopping 70% said they were working on four or more HWW goals (vs. only 33% of non-Transformational Consumers).

These are rolling, ongoing changes. The goals themselves, and what Transformational Consumers do in an effort to reach them, shift, evolve, multiply, and shrink throughout life. What's important is that, in the life of a Transformational Consumer, there is some behavior change goal or goals under way nearly all the time.

I call these rolling, behavior-change projects of the Transformational Consumer personal disruption projects, campaigns, or initiatives.

The Harvard professor Clayton Christensen originally reclaimed the term "disruption" to describe companies that violently transform an industry, because existing industry giants are unwilling or unable to change with the times. A few years later, his colleague Whitney Johnson used the phrase "personal disruption" in talking about individual people building what she described as "disruptive skill sets" and dreaming about how their careers and lives might be different.

The way we use "personal disruption" in the context of the Transformational Consumer is even broader still. These are efforts to change your own behavior with the specific intention to level up your life in any way, to make anything about your life different and better. What's violent about it is that behavior change is hard to do. Really hard, in fact.

Who is a hero? He who conquers his own urges.

—THE TALMUD

Hundreds, maybe even thousands of influences impact whether a given person succeeds at a given personal disruption campaign or whether one is "good" at managing one's own behavior in general. Nature, nurture, personal experiences of trauma and learning, belief systems, skills, resources, current environment, and social set: all of these factors and many more influence a given individual's ability to make desired behavior changes.

To paraphrase Sister Mary Catherine, most people want to make these changes and have a good sense for what it will take. Of course, some personal disruption campaigns involve an initial stage of information gathering, knowledge building, or education. But often people actually know from the very beginning, in a general way, *what* they need to do:

▲ They want to stop doing something dysfunctional, such as over-spending.

▲ They want to start doing something, such as exercising.

▲ They want to accomplish a finite project, such as getting a CPA license or learning a language.

▲ They want to keep doing something they view as beneficial, such as eating a generally healthful diet.

The hard part is for people to actually make themselves do it—to make the change and stick with it. Sticking with your eating plan when you're constantly confronted with pizza at kids' parties and donuts at work is not easy.

And Transformational Consumers know this. Eighty-seven percent said they know that if they can manage their own behavior and habits, they can change their lives, contrasted with only 66% of non-Transformational Consumers who were aware that the Personal Disruption Conundrum is such a powerful limiting factor.

This is a battle royal against a force that encompasses and is somehow even greater than all of the influences and factors I listed earlier, an anti-force that arises in the face of almost any effort to make a life change or behavior change for the healthier, wealthier, and wiser. This is the force of Resistance, with a capital R, and it is the root of the Personal Disruption Conundrum. We'll explore it much more in chapter 2, as we see how it plays out in real life.

M—Have an Extreme Growth (versus Fixed) *Mindset*

The Stanford researcher Carol Dweck says that there are two ways people perceive themselves and what is possible for their lives. She says most people have either a growth mindset or a fixed mindset.[3]

People who have a fixed mindset believe that they are who they are, when it comes to their basic qualities, such as intelligence and talent, from the day they are born. They believe these things are fixed, and there's nothing they can do about it. They are just playing the cards life has dealt them, for better or for worse.

People with growth mindsets, on the other hand, believe that their most essential qualities are subject to change. They believe that they can learn, get better, become smarter, and build new skills and talents. And this is key: they understand that the way they can access new levels of possibility for themselves and their lives is through persistence, work, and development, versus inborn talent or "smarts." People with a growth mindset even view their failures as an opportunity to learn and grow.

Transformational Consumers are extreme growth-mindset people. They believe that everything about themselves and their lives is subject to change for the better, at all times. Eighty-one percent of the Transformational Consumers we surveyed said they believe they can change almost anything about their lives that they want to. Only 55% of non-Transformational Consumers said the same.

Transformational Consumers might not know exactly how to make a specific change, but they believe that change is possible in every area of their lives. They believe their lives are especially changeable for the healthier, wealthier, or wiser: areas in which their own behavior has a clear impact on their outcomes.

They see themselves as people who believe in change and believe in the possible. They view and tell their own life stories through this lens.

And they get excited about helping others change their lot in life, as well.

They are very vocal about their goals and about the services that helped them succeed, online and off. In fact, when they succeed at making a major life transformation, Transformational Consumers tend to trigger the fixed-mindset people around them into wondering whether their lives might really have more growth potential for themselves than they generally believed.

This partly explains why Transformational Consumers are so influential: people like to be around people who are inspirational. In our survey, 58% of Transformational Consumers said that people often seek their advice on how to improve their lives, compared with only 21% of non-Transformational Consumers.

Growth mindset is contagious. Think of the Transformational Consumers in your audience as the outbreak monkeys of this critically important form of social contagion: they help others believe that hard personal disruption can really, truly happen.

A—Possess an Innate or Learned Bias toward *Action*

The truth is, most people would like to be healthier, wealthier, and wiser. But all of those people don't believe they actually can be. And many aren't willing to invest their time and money into a constant series of efforts to make it happen. While "normal" consumers might talk about doing something to improve their HWW, Transformational Consumers exhibit a bias toward doing something about it. I call this a bias toward action.

Eighty-nine percent of Transformational Consumers said that when they are not happy with something in their life, they usually try to do something about it. Compare this with only 70% of non-Transformational Consumers who said the same thing.

Think of it this way: Transformational Consumers don't like to stay stuck.

Now, the action that a specific Transformational Consumer will take to pursue a HWW goal will look different for different individuals and even for the same individual in different areas of his or her life. One might start doing research, while another might hire a coach or trainer. One might set a goal in writing, and yet another might enroll in a workshop.

Some might be stronger at accomplishing health goals than financial goals. They might flounder. They might not do the exact right thing. But they tend not to sit long in situations they are unhappy with without trying to do *something*.

That said, Transformational Consumers can and do get stuck like everyone else. In fact, our data show that they are *more* intimidated by challenges (42%) than average (36%) and non-Transformational Consumers (31%). They experience setbacks, decision traps, and quit points, just like everyone else. They struggle with procrastination, focus, habit making and breaking, and willpower more than most, possibly because they are more likely than others to be trying to make a change at any point in time.

This struggle is precisely why they look for products, tools, and content to help them make changes. It's why they are willing to experiment with things that might help them make progress, why they are early adopters. These sticking points create some of the richest opportunities for Transformer companies to reach and engage Transformational Consumers.

N—Engage in a *Never-Ending* Search to Find Products, Services, and Content That Support Their Behavior-Change Goals

▲ Transformational Consumers want health, wealth, and wisdom.

▲ They know that it'll take self-management to get there—and stay there.

▲ They believe that this sort of behavior change is possible but have found it to be hard.

▲ So they consistently look to brands and businesses for the help they need in making those changes.

    – They come looking for products and services.

    – They come for coaching and training.

    – They come for collaboration.

    – They come for inspiration.

    – They come for illumination.

    – They come looking for ease, joy, and beauty.

    – They come for nuts-and-bolts tools, apps, events, content, opportunities.

    – They come to get in motion. To interrupt their inertia or bad habits. To stay in motion.

And they come looking for these things to every single sector of the marketplace, from advisory services to educational institutions, to travel, leisure, luxury, and personal development, to retail, to food, to consumer packaged goods, and definitely to tech.

In our survey, Transformational Consumers overindexed on using products and content to get healthier, wealthier, and wiser in every way we asked about. And get this: Transformational Consumers were anywhere from five to ten times more likely to engage in Aspiration-driven use of products and content than were non-Transformational Consumers.

Table 3 Comparing the Transformational Product Usage and Consumption Behavior of Transformational, non-Transformational, and Overall Consumers

Q: I use digital products (like apps or websites) or real-world, physical products to help me do the following things, a few times a week or more often:

	Respondents overall (%)	Transformational Consumers (%)	Non-Transformational Consumers (%)
Lose weight	23	42	4
Improve my health	36	63	9
Save or manage my money	40	70	11
Become a better person	36	65	8
Improve or practice a skill	37	65	8
Manage my stress	33	59	6
Learn something new	52	86	18
Explore new cultures	25	45	5

Table 4 Comparing the Transformational Content Consumption Behavior of Transformational, non-Transformational, and Overall Consumers

Q: I read blogs, articles, newsletters, or books to help me learn about the following things, *a few times a week or more often*:

	Respondents overall (%)	Transformational Consumers (%)	Non-Transformational Consumers (%)
Health and fitness	32	57	7
Losing weight	24	43	5
Personal finance	29	52	6
New people, places, or cultures	29	52	6
Self-improvement	31	56	6
A new skill or language	21	39	3
Stress management	25	47	4

Remember, this is the only characteristic that someone *must* possess to qualify as a Transformational Consumer. It breaks down into three elements:

1. The Transformational Consumer's *motivation* for seeking transformational help from the marketplace
2. The marketplace-seeking *behavior* itself
3. The *implications* of that behavior

What qualifies a purchase or other engagement as transformational is one thing and one thing only: the consumer's motivation for making that purchase or interacting with the brand.

The product itself doesn't necessarily have to be a health or financial product. If consumers are engaging with the brand as part of an effort to make their life healthier, wealthier, or wiser *or* if they are choosing to buy one brand over another because they think it's a healthier, wealthier, or wiser choice, we count it as transformational spending or brand engagement.

TCI has developed a Transformational Spending Index, which tracks annual consumer spending across 72 categories. Consumers' likely motivation for making a given type of purchase is what qualifies a particular purchase category for inclusion in the index, which means that this index will never be able to capture 100% of actual transformational spending. Think about it: some portion of people who use, say, dating apps probably do so motivated at least in part by a desire to live a healthier, wealthier, wiser life. Many others probably are motivated by, um, other reasons. So we don't include dating apps and services, even though there's an argument for doing so.

We include in the index only categories of consumer spending, purchases, and sectors that our research or common sense indicates the overwhelming majority of people make based on HWW motivations. And we're okay with the idea that we will always *under*estimate the levels of transformational spending that are taking place.

Our first Transformational Spending Index estimates that consumers spent $4.1 trillion on transformational spending in the United States in 2015 (download the index in full at TransformationalConsumer.com).

I repeat: this is not a niche. A full 60% of U.S. consumer spending reflects transformational spending, and that is calculated very conservatively.

One more thing: many products you would not think of as transformational can be. And on the other hand, *not* every purchase can or should be marketed as transformational or "health washed" in an effort to appeal to Transformational Consumers. Whether a purchase is transformational is determined entirely by whether the customer's motivation for buying it was driven by an HWW goal or Aspiration.

Let's take two different products within the category of household products: soap and garbage bags.

Many soap purchases are *not* transformational. But some are. Unilever, for example, has been selling soap for years in developing countries, with content marketing focused on delivering the message that hand washing prevents disease and saves lives.[4] When customers in these countries buy soap with the motivation of keeping their families healthy and well, those purchases are transformational.

Even in industrialized countries, when people buy one soap versus another because it is natural or nontoxic, their motivation is health, and that's a transformational purchase, too.

But not all soap purchase decisions are.

Contrast the case of soap with that of garbage bags. Very, very few people are motivated by their health when they buy garbage bags. There's a tiny sliver of customers who think about the health of the planet or are buying compostable bags, but to call this product category transformational would strain credibility. So we don't.

How to Think Like a Transformational Consumer

Tech, Tuna, and Toys That Transform

When people first learn about the Transformational Consumer, they very commonly assume that the conversation is limited to health products or financial brands. Not so. The aim of the framework is to get us to start thinking about our customers and their lives and the role we can play in them the same way they do.

They think much more broadly and much more flexibly about how products help them achieve their goals.

The only qualifier on whether a brand could become transformational is (a) whether people buy it in an effort to live healthier, wealthier, or wiser or (b) whether people choose it over another, competing product because it furthers their health, wealth, and wisdom goals. Through this lens, you will find transformation in surprising places:

▲ **Tech.** Obviously, health tech, EdTech, and FinTech companies are often transformational. But so are collaborative-consumption companies like Airbnb and Lyft, which empower people to use their homes and vehicles to make money and change their finances (pay off bills, start a business, etc.).

Lyft's CMO, Kira Wampler, once told me that almost 60% of Lyft drivers in Los Angeles are actually musicians, actors, and artists who say they are able to keep at their creative endeavors because they can make income by driving. Airbnb's head of product, Joe Zadeh, said he sees both the company's hosts and its guests as Transformational Consumers: the guests because they want noncommercial travel experiences that help them develop as people and the hosts because they are putting their real estate resources to their best and highest use.[5]

Most business and consumer office software, such as operating systems, aims to make people more productive at work and manage their time more efficiently, both of which fall under "wealthy" and "wise." And the tech giants are also taking a transformational bent. Google's "Goals" features allows people to dedicate time to their aspirations on their calendars,[6] and Apple has invested billions in reaching Transformational Consumers with the Apple Watch.[7]

▲ **Tuna.** A friend of mine once challenged me about a photo of a woman buying tuna on the TCI website, asking me, "How is tuna helping her achieve her goals?" He was surprised when I shared the survey results that over 35% of Transformational Consumers specify "high-protein" as a guideline for how they try to eat. (Only 17% of non-Transformational Consumers say the same.) Buying a can of tuna may even help a Transformational Consumer achieve such goals as "save money by taking a lunch to work" or "eat better by cooking more at home."

▲ **Toys.** Many parents pick and purchase toys on the basis of educational and developmental features, facilitating their children's developmental health and, arguably, wisdom as well. Both Lego[8] and Disney[9] have deep, secondary businesses that provide education and training for businesspeople, helping them become wealthier and wiser—Google "Lego Serious Play Method" and "Disney Institute."

As business leaders, we often think about what's possible for our businesses by sector and industry, by whether we're a start-up or an incumbent, by whether we operate a brick-and-mortar or are fully online. But Transformational Consumers look at products through the lens of the changes they are trying to make and whether our products can help make them. *That's it.* Don't miss out on the opportunity to reach and engage billions of people worldwide because of your own limited thinking about your business.

From Consumer to Character

The archetypal Transformational Consumer is constantly looking for brands that will help them change their behavior and lives for the healthier, wealthier, and wiser. And when they find those brands, magic happens. Transformational Consumers will be the protagonists of the great company-customer love stories of our time.

But love stories aren't written about archetypes. They are written about characters with rich, nuanced interior and exterior lives.

As characters, Transformational Consumers are real, living, breathing people, with unique visions, skills, and challenges. They are individual human beings, with personal flaws, fears, and dreams.

Contrary to conventional business wisdom, engaging these Transformational Consumers is not about telling a story of your brand or your company. It's about crafting an authentic, relatable, warts-and-all before-and-after story *about them* and delivering products and content that help them progress along their journeys. It's about telling a tale of the transformation that's possible in their lives and about telling it in their own natural language. It's about casting them in the role of hero on their own transformational journey and then providing the resources to make this story come true, over and over, for a lifetime.

CHAPTER TWO

Removing Resistance and Triggering Progress

The first rule of personal finance is that it's not personal and it's not financial. It's about your ability to make ten changes and not get too depressed over it.

—JAMES ALTUCHER

TRANSFORMATIONAL TAKEAWAYS

1. The love and loyalty that a Transformational Consumer gives your brand is directly proportional to the degree of change you help them make or the beauty or ease with which you help them make it.
2. Transformer companies remove resistance, difficulty, frictions, and pain points from a Transformational Consumer's journey.
3. Transformer companies also trigger progress along the transformational journey, by facilitating hard things, activating already motivated people, or functioning as a tool, medium, or social actor.

I won't bury the lede here: the love that Transformational Consumers will have or develop for your brand is directly proportional to the degree of HWW change your company helps them make or the incremental beauty, joy, or ease you add to the journey toward their goals.

Think of every Transformational Consumer's process of pursuing any individual goal as just that: a process, a journey. Depending on the goal or the person, a journey might take a week, 72 days, four years, or a lifetime. All along the journey toward every HWW goal that our intrepid aspirants ever attempt, they will encounter two categories of phenomena: resistance and progress triggers. I often refer to these categories as things that get people stuck (resistance) and unstuck (progress triggers).

By definition, Transformers are the companies that remove resistance and trigger progress at critical moments along the journeys of the people they serve.

Resistance

Resistance includes any and every manner of emotional pushback, decision trap, logistical difficulty, ability hurdle, pain point, friction, or psychological bias that causes people to stumble, get stuck, get frustrated, or flat-out quit along their goal journey. Resistance is the root of the Personal Disruption Conundrum, that sense that people know what they should be doing to change their behavior for the healthier, wealthier, and wiser but can't seem to make themselves actually do it.

Every field of human behavior studies this resistance, though they all call it something different. Behavioral economists talk about fallacies and biases. Behavioral psychologists talk about the hurdles to habit formation and the hardness of willpower. Product designers and technologists talk about "friction"[1] or "pain points."[2] Tim Ferriss calls them "failure points."[3]

Psychoanalysts, spiritual teachers, and philosophers talk about how the ego creates "psychological resistance" to our efforts to break dysfunctional patterns and build optimal, new ones. In 1904, Freud himself wrote that "psychoanalytic treatment may in general be conceived of as such a re-education in overcoming internal resistances." This concept only grew in its centrality to his work. By 1926, he had catalogued five different formats of resistance: repression, transference, gain from illness (secondary gains from dysfunctional behavior), the repression compulsion (repeating difficult, distressing, or traumatic behavior patterns), and self-sabotage—and characterized the work of psychoanalysis as a slow "working-through" all of these types of resistance.[4]

The creativity guru and modern philosopher Steven Pressfield has written prolifically on what he calls Resistance, with a capital R, noting that it arises in reaction to "any act that rejects immediate gratification in favor of long-term growth, health, or integrity." In one of several books on how to release Resistance, he first describes it as a universal element of human experience. "We're wrong if we think we're the only ones struggling with Resistance," Pressfield writes. "Everyone who has a body experiences Resistance."[5]

Pressfield goes so far as to personify Resistance, writing about it as a villain with human-like traits and motives, including one overarching goal. "Resistance," he writes "aims to kill . . . our genius, our soul, the unique and priceless gift we were put on this earth to give and that no one else has but us."[6] This characterization is decidedly consistent with my personal and professional observations of how Transformational Consumers experience Resistance. Resistance is not futile. *Resistance is fatal.* In the minds of the Transformational Consumer, across a lifetime of unsuccessfully trying to make desperately desired life and behavior changes, Resistance can extinguish the spark of desire for the healthier, happier, more prosperous, more self-actualized life that these people want. Resistance can kill the dreams, beliefs, and bias toward action that are so elemental to the spirit of people who were once motivated and on a mission to be their highest and best selves and live their highest and best lives.

Being repeatedly stymied from reaching their most desired dreams by Resistance can traumatize people, especially those who run into it over and over again, without finding a way to overcome it, and especially when the dream is something as emotionally and culturally loaded as what you earn or how much you weigh.

In a post on the deep-thought blog *Medium* titled "How I Learned to Give Dieting the Middle Finger," the radio journalist Jacquie Fuller shares an extraordinarily common, extraordinarily traumatic experience of Transformational Consumers who have butted up against Resistance to making long-term health changes repeatedly, over a lifetime. This particular experience is so common that it has a name in pop culture: the yo-yo diet.

> Throughout the '80s and '90s and pretty much until the day I walked into The Emily Program, I was the poster child for yo-yo dieting. In the '80s, I actually ate an AYDS bar (remember those? I didn't think so.) I brought a lunch of plain tuna on rice cakes to high school for months. In the '90's, I took Formula One until my heart felt like it was going to fly out of my chest. Over two decades, I intermittently Weight Watched my way from Exchanges to Points to PointsPlus. I Slim Fasted, South Beached, Atkinsed, Paleoed. I saw holistic nutritionists. I did pretty much everything except that one diet that's all cookies because that sounded fucking stupid. In addition to the countless diets, lapsed gym memberships littered my past like bodies on a battlefield. (If you could lay them end to end, you'd have two lifetime memberships.) . . .
>
> Dieting. Then not dieting. Then dieting again. Dieting, but wishing I could just eat like everybody else—without counting, weighing, planning, always always thinking about food. I was obsessed with food, but didn't want to be. I was in a constant state of restriction—declaring the food-villain-du-jour (fat, sugar, gluten) as off-limits, then pretty much falling face-first into a vat of it. I need a t-shirt that says "I spent a near-lifetime sprinkling steamed vegetables with Molly McButter, and all I got was this t-shirt and a general feeling of WHITE HOT RAGE."

But then Fuller hit a turning point. As she told about the therapists that helped her heal from a lifetime of this Resistance-induced trauma, she wrote,

> One of the first assignments given to me in treatment was to eat dessert. Sounds simple enough, but every cell in my body recoiled at the sugges-

tion. It wasn't until I did this—ate dessert because a licensed, trained psychologist *told me to*—that I realized it had been years since I'd truly *enjoyed* dessert. I baked a fresh batch of chocolate chip cookies, sat at the table with a glass of milk, and ate them slowly. I felt a veritable parade of emotions march through me—elation, fear, panic, contentment, sadness. I may have cried. And at the end of it, I felt a fullness that was only partly physical. I felt like I didn't need another cookie. In that moment, or for a long time. Someone had thrown wide-open the once-locked cookie cabinet, and suddenly knowing I could go in there *any time I wanted*, diminished my desire.

I probably owe [the program] my life. I definitely owe it my joy.

Fuller went on to describe the founder of the program that finally helped her get off the diet roller coaster. In doing so, Fuller explained that the founder was "sketch" and her fashion sense objectionable before adding, "I'd like to kiss her. Like, hard." She went on: "This program works. (For me.) Despite 10 weeks of insufferable videos, I've lost weight with so *little* suffering, my spouse actually remarked upon it ("I haven't heard you complain at all.")."[7]

When your product, service, or content helps a Transformational Consumer heal from that trauma and (finally) remove impeding Resistance from his or her journey, your brand becomes a Transformer. And the more Resistance you remove, the easier you make progress, and the more pain and friction you remove from the journey, the more love and engagement that person will have for your product or company.

Progress Triggers

Your company can trigger transformational progress in just as many ways as Resistance can impede it. By no means are the following guideposts and examples exhaustive, but I hope they will start to expand the ways you think about companies helping their customers make transformational progress.

Facilitate with Knowledge

I often hear aspiring Transformer companies say they aim to educate their audiences with content marketing that delivers a ton of information about their goals and how to achieve them. My two cents is that information is just data, and there's no shortage of that in the lives of Transformational Consumers. In fact, at this stage of the Internet, more information always threatens to overwhelm or distract this audience.

Knowledge, however, is information strategically configured and delivered to solve a specific problem or challenge people face. Many Transformer companies have built thriving product lines and brilliant marketing programs around knowledge solutions to HWW problems or challenges.

The *Mint Life* blog is one of the best examples of such a program, triggering Mint users' progress toward financial goals like saving money toward a goal and getting out of debt with content that creates aha moments and powers progress. A post titled "The 50/20/30 Rule for Minimalist Budgeting," for example, helps younger Mint users overcome the frustration with complex budget plans by offering a basic budget outline that assigns 50% of income to expenses, 20% to savings, and 30% to personal lifestyle line items such as dinners out and the like.[8]

The Mint team credits the blog for the program's early adoption and continued traffic momentum of over 13 million visitors per month, almost ten years after the blog's beginnings.[9] In an interview with *Kissmetrics Blog*, Mint's former lead designer flat-out called it: "Our app didn't have a high viral coefficient, but we had content that [did]."[10]

This sort of knowledge facilitates customers' transformational progress by providing clarity and direction for what to do next: the just-right knowledge, in the just-right format, in the just-right time and place in their journeys.

Activate

Products and content can also activate customers who are already very motivated to take a specific, timely action wherever they happen to be on the web or in the world, something the Stanford computer-science professor B. J. Fogg calls "putting a hot trigger in the path."[11]

A push notification to go for a run 30 minutes before the time a customer has logged runs in the past? That's a hot trigger, placed in the customer's path. Sending an April 14th email to investors who haven't yet funded their IRAs, with a link to where they can do so and a reminder that the deadline is less than 24 hours away? That's putting a hot trigger in the customer's path.

You can also serve up activation via inspiration. People who are just embarking on a transformational journey (and people who have gotten stuck along the way) can often be reactivated with a spark of inspiration, small or large. On the small side, many companies publish inspirational quotes and mantras on social media channels, primarily because Transformational Consumers love that little kick-start of activation for a long week of entrepreneurial challenges or health/wealth self-discipline.

Content programs that reposition difficult parts of a transformational journey as more fun, beautiful, or enjoyable than they have seemed before can also be activating. Business and financial challenges (debt, diets, etc.), fitness challenges, and healthy recipe programs featuring gorgeously plated meal pics all fit this bill: inspiration-cum-activation.

On the large side, whole content programs, user success stories, and testimonial programs can be crafted with activation as the top-line objective. When the marketing technology vendor Marketo asked me to speak to business audiences around the world about how I'd used their software to grow a blog audience of over ten million people in less than a year, the idea was not just to explain the software's features. The goal was to inspire people to believe that level of achievement was possible for them and their businesses, too. In delivering these talks, my goal was to help the marketers in the audience become unstuck and inspired with new ideas, beliefs, and yes, ultimately, the software as a tool they could use to execute their own marketing and business goals. (It's worth noting here that Transformational Consumers frequently look to B2B products and software for help making progress on their wealthy and wise goals).

Persuasive Roles: Tool, Medium, Social Actor

At Stanford, B. J. Fogg also developed a framework for how computers and technology can be used to change how people act and think by serving three "persuasive roles" he deems the Functional Triad: tool, medium, and social actor.[12] I take this idea even further: this framework suggests how companies in any sector, online or off and even including professional services, food, and consumer packaged goods companies, can think about inserting progress triggers into their customers' journeys.

Tool. When your brand or company acts as a Tool, you increase your customers' *capability* to do things in one of a few ways.[13] It might make the behavior they want to do logistically faster, financially cheaper, or physically easier to do. It might lead them through a step-by-step process that eliminates complexity and reduces the number of brain cycles. Or it might perform calculations or measurements that spike your hero-customers' level of motivation.

Think about your bank's app or your online investment dashboard. Tools. The software you'd use to organize your small company's finances or the software your gym uses for you to register for classes? Tools. Think about the organic foods you buy and healthy snacks: also Tools. In fact, most athletic apparel, healthy food, and even things such as finance, fitness, and mindfulness apps that show you just how much money you've saved, how many miles you've cycled, and how many times you've meditated this year also fall within this Tool category.

Medium. As a Medium, your company provides *experiences* that help create transformation, by helping people learn cause-and-effect relationships, as MyFitnessPal does by helping people learn which foods and eating habits create weight gain and which do the reverse. According to Fogg, media also "provide[s] people with vicarious experiences that motivate" them (à la user success stories) and "help people rehearse a behavior."[14]

Inserting mindfulness into the loop of habitual or automatic decisions, with behavior tracking, logging, notifications, and emails, is one powerful strategy that Medium apps and businesses use to help people break habits.

Social actor. Transformer companies that play the role of social actor enable *relationships* that help create behavior change. Originally, Fogg wrote about social actors as computers that interacted in human-like, personal ways with their users.[15] But that was all before social media even existed.

In the context of Transformational Consumers, social actor companies that connect customers with each other via such social features as friend feeds, messaging tools, leaderboards, hashtag campaigns, and discussion boards may all set the stage for your customers to experience positive behavior change. Companies also serve as behavior-changing social actors when they host live events such as classes, workshops, and clubs; via product ratings and reviews; and by hosting and creating social media conversations between customers with similar aspirations.

Transformer Beware: The Dangers of Trying to Motivate the Unmotivated

Professor Fogg says there are only three elements that must exist for a behavior to change: motivation, ability, and a trigger. It is extremely difficult, maybe even impossible, to motivate the unmotivated. It is a much more fruitful endeavor to find motivated people and make their desired changes easier (increase ability) or help activate them (put a hot trigger in their path).

In chapter 6, "Rethink Your Customer," you'll learn about how to map out the journeys of your already motivated customers, empowering your products and content to meet them where they are.

Consider this beloved quote of Transformational Consumers everywhere:

Until one is committed, there is hesitancy, the chance to draw back, always ineffectiveness. Concerning all acts of initiative (and creation), there is one elementary truth the ignorance of which kills countless ideas and splendid plans: that the moment one definitely commits oneself, then Providence moves too. All sorts of things occur to help one that would never otherwise have occurred. A whole stream of events issues from the decision, raising in one's favor all manner of unforeseen incidents and meetings and material assistance, which no man could have dreamed would have come his way. Whatever you can do, or dream you can do, begin it. Boldness has genius, power, and magic in it. Begin it now.

—WILLIAM H. MURRAY

Yes, Resistance is real. But I read this quote as paying homage to the cosmic counterforce to Resistance. When you become a Transformer company, you reposition your business as producer of the exact sorts of events, incidents, and material assistance your Transformational Consumer audience needs to encounter in order to make progress on their journey. You reposition and rethink the very things you sell, your every marketing message, fashioning them into the "sorts of things that occur" to help Transformational Consumers who have set out on their own quests for healthier, wealthier, wiser lives.

CHAPTER THREE

The Hero's Journey of Your Transformational Consumer

There ain't no journey what don't change you some.

—DAVID MITCHELL

> **TRANSFORMATIONAL TAKEAWAYS**
>
> 1. Each of a Transformational Consumer's HWW goals represents a quest that plays out along the same format as the age-old Hero's Journey story line.
> 2. Your company's role is mentor, aide, guide, or tool (including supplies) on your customer-hero's quest.
> 3. The quests of Transformational Consumers unfold in complex yet predictable ways: they are rarely logical or linear, they overlap with each other, one quest often snowballs into another, and they are fueled by social contagion.

It's illuminating to think of a Transformational Consumer's journey toward achieving any individual HWW goal as unfolding along the story line of the Hero's Journey. In case you're not familiar with it, the Hero's Journey is an archetypal story model, a recurring story pattern that human beings have been telling, hearing, reading, and watching since the beginning of time.

In a Hero's Journey, as explained by Joseph Campbell, who first identified the universality of this story line, "a hero ventures forth from the world of common day into a region of supernatural wonder: fabulous forces are there encountered and a decisive victory is won: the hero comes back from this mysterious adventure with the power to bestow boons on his fellow man."[1]

Story experts and mythologists have unpacked the universal Hero's Journey into a long list of sequential steps and elements. (If you'd like to dive deeper, I encourage you to read Christopher Booker's *The Seven Basic*

Plots: Why We Tell Stories.)[2] For our purposes, though, the most important elements of the Hero's Journey include

▲ The hero (your customer)

▲ A quest for transformation that involves a journey away from everything the hero has ever known (life, health, prosperity, or personal growth goal; aim to change from the status quo), in which the hero encounters

▲ Enemies and villains (Resistance of all sorts)

▲ Mentors, allies, guides, or tools (these can be lots of things, including your company, your product, your services, your content, etc.)

▲ A battle and victory (progress of all sorts, including behavior change or completion of a goal)

▲ The return home, as a changed being, with new skills, resources, and assets (your customers' healthier, wealthier, wiser life *and* newfound momentum, confidence, and knowledge of how to change things in their lives).

This archetypal story is encoded in our collective human memory, our cells, and our neurons. Nearly every Bible story, fairy tale fable, and even most modern movies and media narratives unfold along this plotline. Jesus Christ, Luke Skywalker, Harriett Tubman, Nelson Mandela, and Erin Brockovich: these all count as heroes whose journeys we know, whether or not we love them.

Let's take a deeper look at a few individual Transformational Consumers and their effort to pursue some of the most common HWW goals of Transformational Consumers. Watch how these journeys unfold along the same story points as the Hero's Journey. You'll soon begin to see how companies like yours can and do help Transformational Consumers vanquish the villain of Resistance and make progress on their quests, achieving the most important objectives of the business in the process.

Latent in your hero-customers' journeys are all sorts of untapped possibilities for ways you can help them make progress, pointing you to opportunities for innovation, new product features, and marketing messages and campaigns. But to get that value from the journey, you must first unlimit your thinking about what's allowed beyond the obvious, expanding your own universe of what you understand as permissible or possible ways for a company to be a mentor, ally, guide, or tool.

Note that the role of Transformer companies in these Transformational Consumers' hero-customer quests generally aligns to the role of mentor, ally, guide, or tool. Mentors, allies, and guides tend to be service providers or content programs. They are more likely to be local businesses than tools are. In fact, if your business is your own personal services as a coach, therapist, personal trainer, financial planner, real estate broker, retreat producer, or health-care provider, you yourself might literally be your hero-customer's mentor, ally, or guide.

Beyond the obvious, there are a couple of ways in which Transformer companies serve these roles for Transformational Consumers that are much subtler but represent *most* of Transformational Consumer spending and brand interactions along their HWW journeys. Apps, platforms, and even brand-published content can serve as a tool with which your hero-customers ultimately unlimits themselves into their transformed life.

The tools you can provide to help power your customer-heroes' journeys also include *supplies*. The transformational journey can be uncomfortable; by definition, it involves a journey away from what's known, a change from the status quo, a foray away from the dopamine-fueled comforts of loafing, inertia, bad habits, and salty, sugary, fatty convenience foods. It almost always involves more work than the status quo did.

An enormous portion of what Transformational Consumers are constantly on the lookout for is new, beneficial versions of the old things they used to buy—supplies for the new version of their life that they are still likely to eat or use but are more healthful, are more financially frugal or efficient or luxurious, and/or that represent or enable smarter decisions than the old versions did. Think of supplies as tools to *sustain* transformation: supplies that customers can bring back with them to stay on track in their newly transformed lives. This is a powerful way that consumer packaged goods, food, and apparel companies can fulfill their potential to become Transformers.

One more note: while these stories might strike you as extreme, they are actually compilations of real-life stories of Transformational Consumers from our research, online listening, and our lives.

Christopher: A Customer-Hero's Journey to Healthier

Christopher, a 46-year-old financial officer, had been an athlete in high school and still thought of himself that way. But like so many others, he found himself in a desk job after college. Weekends were spent with the kids, and the pounds piled on. His doctor had mentioned that he should get some sort of fitness routine going, and he had tried running—he even joined a gym a couple of years back. He was still paying the gym dues but only made it there maybe once or twice a month, in a fit of inspiration. He told himself he'd go back after he closed this big deal. But there always seemed to be another big deal on its tail.

Then four small, but extraordinary, things happened in a single week.

On Friday, the doctor's office rang to say that Christopher's blood work showed that he was prediabetic. Christopher immediately turned to Google and started reading about how many people believed that different diets could reverse prediabetes. This gave him some level of hope. He ate a salad that night but gave into the temptation of dessert.

On Saturday, he pulled on some old running gear and realized he was completely out of breath less than two blocks from home. Ugh.

On Sunday at church, he caught a glimpse of himself in the window as he walked up and was actually startled at the not-at-all-distorted image of himself. He couldn't really believe that overweight, middle-age man had replaced the youthful athlete he still saw in his mental mirror. Restrictive diets don't work, he told himself as he helped himself to a second helping of scalloped potatoes at Sunday brunch.

On Monday, he got a Facebook message from an old work friend who was back in town, asking to meet up for a drink after work. Excited to see his old friend, Christopher went to meet him at the pub and was shocked and stunned to see his friend looking so trim and full of energy. He looked younger than he had five years ago. His friend mentioned having done an AIDS Lifecycle (ALC) bike ride from Chicago to Minneapolis a few years back, after losing a friend to AIDS. That had kick-started a new way of life.

Heading back to the office, Christopher was pensive, opting to take the stairs, which he knew was the healthy choice, despite having rarely chosen it. As he huffed and puffed his way up the stairs, wondering when they added all those extra flights between the ground and his office, he knew one thing for sure: if his friend could do that bike ride, he could do it, too.

Christopher was a competitive guy. Seeing his friend in such fine mettle had reignited that spark. He decided it was about time he harnessed that energy into something that was good for himself, not just for making money (though he liked making money plenty). It was also so much more energizing to think about setting a goal of doing this ride than thinking about managing blood-sugar levels or hitting a goal weight. So the same night as he saw his friend, he mentioned it to his wife and then, before he went to sleep, Googled "AIDS Lifecycle" on his iPad.

Christopher went to the orientation for the bike ride and realized that the time commitment was not insignificant: every Saturday, most of the day, for what boiled down to the first month of the year. He'd also have to raise several thousand dollars for charity. The nearest ride to his home was from San Francisco to Los Angeles. After talking with his family, who were excited at his enthusiasm and the prospect of him taking better care of himself, he made a decision to throw himself into this for six months and signed up.

The next step was to gear up. The ALC trainers gave him a list of gear he'd need, and he spent a Saturday with his kids at the local sports super-store getting everything. He downloaded Strava, the cycling app, and MyFitnessPal and synced the two. He got a huge rush from watching the cumulative annual miles ridden on Strava rack up.

Almost immediately, once he started training and tracking, his craving for soda disappeared, and he also cut his alcohol consumption once he logged a beer and realized it had the same number of calories as he'd just burned on a two-hour bike ride he'd just completed. He got really into prepping meals on the weekend for work, and his wife joined him. They also made some simple household food rules, like this: that they could have a drink or eat dessert anytime they wanted when they were out but would not stock ice cream or alcohol in the house.

This health thing had officially become a family affair.

Christopher's energy levels came up, and while he was very occupied with training on the weekends, he felt like he was having more fun with his kids the rest of the time. He felt mentally quicker and just lighter. In fact, he was, having lost 30 pounds in the first 90 days of training. He hadn't weighed himself, so he didn't even realize he'd lost that much weight. His doctor pointed it out when he came in to revisit the prediabetes, which had also resolved. That realization was a big morale and momentum boost, as were the comments made by his friends on MyFitnessPal and Facebook, as he shared the link to his fund-raising page for the ride.

He began to look forward to his weekend training sessions and to see-ing the other people in his training cohort. When his knee began to bother him, a few other guys suggested he cross-train and invited him to come to Crossfit with them. He went and ultimately got his wife to become a Cross-fitter, too. They both started experimenting with the Paleo diet and even started reading up on "ancestral health" online.

Christopher and his wife decided that they would set up a whole-family reward for making it through the intense training schedule when the ride was done and spent a few weeks emailing each other links from Jetsetter, TripAdvisor, and Airbnb. They ultimately decided they wanted to expose their kids to new cultures and to service, so they signed on to their church's mission trip to Peru, which they would follow with a summer vacation through the rain forest and to Machu Picchu.

From January to June, Christopher worked up to be ready for the seven-day, 600-mile ride. He felt very supported and almost no anxiety about the ride itself, given the incredible logistics machine that the folks running the ride had put together and the organization they had already demonstrated throughout the months of training.

On ride day, just before Christopher left home, he dropped a Facebook message to his old work buddy sharing about some other things he'd dropped, thanks, in part, to his friend's example: 50 pounds, prediabetes, and a sedentary family lifestyle. After the ride and the trip, both of which were life changing, Christopher found himself excited to see his friends at Crossfit, and he and his wife were home less than a week before they were plugged right back into those workouts.

Terese: A Customer-Hero's Journey to Wealthier

Terese is a 37-year-old single mom. She was a paralegal until recently. After her divorce, she decided to pursue the dream of being a lawyer that she'd given up when she had her kids 15 years ago. She went back to law school, spent five years completing a part-time program, and just recently graduated.

After Terese passed the bar exam, she secured an attorney job at the same firm she'd worked at for ten years as a paralegal. Once she saw her first paycheck and, more importantly, how much had been withheld for taxes, she asked her Facebook friends for a referral to a CPA and a financial planner, both of whom had the same advice: it's time to buy a house. The mortgage-interest deduction would be a great boost to affordability, and for the first time ever, her kids could walk to school and stop bickering about sharing a room.

Terese had owned a home with her husband but not on her own. She'd actually always had a tendency to buy lots of clothes and dinners out, so she wasn't even sure she could afford to do this. First thing, she mentioned her plan to her parents, who gave her $10,000 toward her down payment. (That made exactly $10,000 she had to put down!) She asked her Facebook friends (again) for their real estate broker recommendations and called up a couple. They told her she needed to get preapproved for a loan, and she spoke with the mortgage broker whom a couple had recommended.

That call was illuminating, if a bit distressing. Terese's income was stellar, but her credit history was troubled. Some credit-card bills had fallen through the cracks during the divorce, and a couple were in collections. Those needed resolving, and her credit score was about 100 points lower than it needed to be to qualify for a mortgage. The mortgage broker also told her that she needed to save up another $50,000 or $75,000 to buy the sort of home she wanted in the sort of area she wanted, as well as establishing some credit accounts on her own and keeping them in good standing for a while.

The first thing she did was to Google around looking first for fast work-arounds. But most other folks on the frugality subreddit discussion board agreed with her mortgage broker that a quick fix was not the answer to these issues. So she started searching the web to learn how others had tackled these projects. For a couple of months, she lagged. It just seemed like too much to take on, on top of everything else she was dealing with. Then one day a friend, a single woman she knew, invited Terese to her housewarming party. And that flicked a mental switch.

Terese decided to get organized, do some math, and set up a timeline. She went to Mint and set up a dashboard, putting her checking, savings, and credit-card accounts online. She set up a "save for a house" goal in Mint, targeting a $75,000 savings target, on top of the money her parents had given her.

She realized it would take her about two years to save that cash at her current spend rate, but she could do it six months faster if she cut out about $1,500 in monthly expenses, which Mint showed she could do by cutting down on eating out and prepared foods and her personal-trainer bill. She made a commitment to cook more at home and spent some time educating herself on meal planning, meal preparation, and recipes, all online. She got organized and systematic about her grocery lists and also started a family outing to the farmer's market every week (where organics were much cheaper, she'd learned).

She teamed up with a few other moms in her neighborhood to do a weekly slow-cooker club, which required her to first buy a slow cooker! She ordered it, along with a couple of healthy slow-cooker cookbooks, on Amazon. She also invested in all-new glass food storage when some of the other moms scoffed at her plasticware, urging her to research BPA leaching online. That took her down an Internet rabbit hole in which she educated herself about phthalates, parabens, and other toxins. She spent the next weekend throwing out old bath washes and replacing them with Dr. Bronner's liquid castile soap, tossing out all sorts of household cleaners and restocking them with Seventh Generation and Method, and replacing body products and cosmetics with coconut oil and natural counterparts.

That same weekend, she searched Yelp to find a few new group exercise studios in the area, ultimately signing up for ClassPass once she realized it would allow her limitless access to boutique fitness studios for the same price as two of her trainer sessions.

She went to CreditKarma.com, which she'd read about on a number of blogs online. She pulled her credit scores and started working on them, first contacting the collection agencies and paying off those accounts, disputing a few inaccuracies, and finally, finding a couple of credit cards she could use to rebuild her own credit, sans husband.

She spent a little time thinking about what she could do to bring more cash in, too. In the process, she met with her family lawyer and realized she had agreed to way less child support than she was entitled to, under the law of her state. Despite her dread of the conversation, she scheduled a meeting with her ex-husband, and he agreed to pay several hundred dollars more every month. Emboldened by her successful foray into speaking up for herself, she also went to Hired and Glassdoor to compare her salary against others but found that her salary was in line with other first-year attorneys. At a friend's suggestion, she even looked at how people made money on Airbnb, concluding that when she was ready, she would aim to buy a duplex so she could rent the other unit out as an Airbnb host, which would free up a little cash so she didn't have to live on such a tight budget.

Before long, Terese's go-to apps were Mint, where she'd check her rapidly accelerating goal progress; Houzz, where she'd fantasize about home styles and decor to stay inspired; and Pinterest, where she also pinned home-design fantasies and recipes. She was constantly on Trulia and Zillow, which she'd pop open all the time to keep track of home-price trends and just to see what was for sale in her dream neighborhoods at any given moment in time. She even went to open houses on the weekends.

She continued working with the financial planner and CPA, who helped her create an estate plan, secure life and disability insurance, and open her first ever retirement accounts while she was working on getting ready to buy a home. They also encouraged her to meet with a banker at her regular bank, who offered her a secured credit card that helped her credit score advance faster, too.

Almost exactly 18 months after her first conversation with the mortgage broker, Credit Karma indicated that her score had hit its target. She reconnected with the mortgage broker, got preapproved, and started house hunting in earnest, becoming a home owner six months later. She didn't buy a duplex, but she did buy a home with a tiny house in the backyard that she rented out on Airbnb when the kids were with their dad.

Having come through so much to get there, she felt like Superwoman, like she could do anything. After devoting a few months to getting the house furnished to her liking and getting the kids settled into school, Terese started itching to tackle another big goal. She'd always wanted to run a marathon, actually.

Giulia: A Customer-Hero's Journey to Wiser

Giulia is a 31-year-old midlevel manager at a major tech company. She grew up in Colorado and has always been smarter than the average bear. During her first job after college, from which she was the first in her family to graduate, she quickly realized that a career path of lifelong growth would be possible only in a bigger market. So she moved to the West Coast and got a job at an agency and then took an in-house marketing job.

Lately, Giulia had been feeling a low-grade, steady state of frustration and stuckness at work. She knew it's normal to have the so-called Sunday-night blues, but lately it'd been more like a feeling of anxiety, depression, and terror than a reluctance to see the recreation of the weekend come to a close. She chalked some of it up to changes at work: she got into her new company when the awesome little start-up she worked for was acquired by the big behemoth, and she was feeling disempowered by being one of thousands of employees where she was once one of hundreds. She'd been struggling to make the case for the resources she needed to do the projects she'd been assigned to do and was feeling unheard and disrespected.

She was also struggling with the feeling that it was her job to market something she didn't care about and didn't believe in, that all she did for a living was to help an already big, already profitable company make even more money.

Giulia kept saying to her friends that she felt like there had to be more out there for her than this. She was well paid and was not really motivated by trying to make more money. She just felt like she was marking time and was definitely not doing what she was put here on the planet to do. She knew she is very smart but also had no idea what she would like to do with the next season of her career. She felt like she might not be qualified to do anything but what she was already doing, for a company similar to the one she worked at. She would've liked to feel like she was working on something that would help people or change their lives.

Then she clicked on a Business Insider post that came up in her Facebook feed, titled "10 Signs It's Time to Quit Your Day Job." Immediately thereafter, she spent an hour sprucing up her LinkedIn profile and browsing the job listings suggested by the site, without consciously realizing what she was doing. She felt nervous but also excited and in that moment decided she was going to make some moves to quit her hated day job and level up her career.

She decided to gear up for this big move the way she had for other big moves she'd made in life. She went back to the yoga class she used to go to regularly, because it made her feel calmer and more grounded, soothing her job-related feelings of being trapped and aimless. She also started using her Headspace app again, using it to get back into the calming habit of meditating ten minutes every morning.

After just a couple of days of that, she spent some time after dinner a few nights messing around on her company's internal job site, on LinkedIn, and on Google, letting her mind kind of run free envisioning different scenarios for her next career season. Maybe she'd start a business or change careers entirely; she'd always been interested in health, actually. Maybe she could be a personal trainer or work for a health company. She wasn't sure, but after searching "career change" online, she ordered Martha Beck's book *Finding Your Way in a Wild New World: Reclaim Your True Nature to Create the Life You Want* and started working her way through it.[3]

Her insurance covered therapy, so she signed up for ten sessions with a therapist who was also a certified career coach to help her get an organized game plan in place. The coach encouraged her to sign up for an eCourse on starting a small business, which she had always been interested in. At the same time, she got her company to cover her tuition for a digital-marketing course at General Assembly, and she started investigating both an MBA program and a yoga-teacher training that would take place later in the year. (She found all of these on Google and voraciously read the reviews before signing up.)

She also started attending more conferences and meet-ups in her town, even on topics she wasn't particularly interested in. With her coach's help, she practiced a little elevator pitch and started introducing herself to interesting people she met at these events, including some of the speakers. She also started asking her friends to keep an eye out for opportunities for her. She told them she was looking for a role in which she felt like her work would be valued internally, while also making a difference in the world.

One of the speakers she met was hosting a career-development retreat, which she decided to splurge on in the name of "investing in" herself. There, she got clear that she wasn't really interested in working as a solopreneur, except maybe as a side business sometime down the road. She went ahead and enrolled in the yoga-teacher training as a way to cultivate her presentation and speaking skills while staying grounded and learning about the body in the process. To boost her confidence, she went shopping online for a new yoga mat and a few new pieces of yoga clothing, discovering that one of her favorite brands, lululemon, had an extensive digital-content marketing program, including a blog she loved.

She thrived in the digital-marketing course and started applying for jobs using those skills at her current company and others. She emailed the other women she'd met at the career retreat, telling them what she was looking for and including a short list of a few companies she was particularly interested in working for in case they knew anyone at any of them. One of those women ultimately introduced her to a hiring manager at lululemon.

She landed a job producing digital content for the company, a role that had a clear and exciting upward path. In her new role, she made time to do some occasional speaking and writing blogs about her transition into a career she loved and even taught a few yoga classes a week. She settled into her new role with a new level of confidence in her ability to speak up and be heard at work and in life and a new level of joy about her ability to make moves, any time she needs to.

Takeaways for Your Transformational Consumers' Journeys

There are a number of things you can take away from these example customer-hero journeys for your own company's journey to becoming a beloved mentor, ally, guide, or tool of the Transformational Consumer.

Transformational Journeys Are Not Always Logical or Linear

These journeys occur in stages that you can see repeated over and over again. In simplifying them, I've made them more linear than they are in real life. The psychotherapist David Richo says that both the archetypal and the real-life "heroic journey is not a move from point A to point B as in football, where the purpose is to go from the line of scrimmage to the goal. It is a movement from point A to point A to the thousandth power, as in baseball, where the purpose is to go from home to home with a point made—that is, something to show for the journey."[4]

Your hero-customer's quest and return goes from their lives and selves and back to their lives and selves. When they return, they return with transformation, new habits, new character, new skills, new capabilities, and new discipline *in addition to* their newly increased health, wealth, and wisdom. But Richo helps us see that the quest and return are not linear, not in a standard Hero's Journey and not in our Customer-Hero's Journey. These journeys may include offshoot journeys, pauses, setbacks, and backtracks or progress spurts. Our customer-heroes might not like to admit it, but they are human. And human behaviors, habits, and behavior change rarely operate on clear logic.

Don't fall into the trap of thinking you have a logical solution to a behavioral, transformational problem, so it's certain to work. I know companies that offer logical solutions to prediabetes without taking into account that if it were that simple for people to change their eating habits, they wouldn't be prediabetic in the first place.

Transformational Consumer Goals Frequently Change, Expand, Shrink, and Proliferate

Goals can range from lowering cholesterol to riding 545 miles down the California coast. Dealing with prediabetes should be the easier of these two, but the energy, enthusiasm, motivation, and competitive spark in the ride is what ultimately made the change and carried the day.

HWW Transformational Goals and Journeys Often Overlap, Snowball, and Spread to Other People in Your Customer-Hero's Life

Hard-won success on one goal, like getting out of debt, creates momentum that adds fuel to the baby motivational fire on another goal, such as cooking more at home. Many Transformational Consumers will be engaged in multiple personal disruption goals and efforts at the same time, and the motivational fire from one can fuel the other. The opposite can also be true. When struggling to make progress on one very important goal, some Transformational Consumers will intentionally shut down others to focus on the one that matters the most.

Beyond running a lot of concurrent goals and personal disruption campaigns, the momentum from one mission accomplished can fuel the next goal. The customer-hero has learned that his or her capacity is greater than he or she might have thought and that the realm of possibility is larger than it was before. And he or she takes that expanded belief system and skill set into the future, into new goals and projects. Ask any real estate agent: it's very common for people who buy homes to lose weight or change jobs in the months after closing.

This transformational snowball effect manifests itself in all sorts of niches. The *New York Times* reported that people who thrive on a Paleo diet are likely to experiment with other "ancestral health" principles in other areas of their lives. If this diet worked for helping them get control over what they put in their bodies, the thinking goes, maybe it'll work for what they put on their bodies and demand from their bodies, too. They go from eating a grain-free diet to wearing goggles that block certain spectra of screen light and even giving up their unnatural work hours and night jobs (cavemen did not work the graveyard shift).[5]

The Force of Relationship Powers Many
Transformational Goals

Each of these stories illustrates one of the most powerful forces in transformation of every sort: relationship. Your customer-hero's mentors, guides, and allies are often people in or through their own social circles who inspire them to go after their goals by virtue of professional advice, competition, accountability, or just sheer partnership. We very often hear from Transformational Consumers that their original acceptance of a given HWW quest took place only after someone they knew was successful at the same thing, like Christopher's friend who'd gotten fit by doing the ALC ride.

Social contagion is real. People need to connect with each other, and it seems that the discomfort of behavior change is often soothed and made manageable when we connect with others who are making the same changes or are engaged in the activities we aspire to make habitual. This is why boutique exercise studios, workplace fitness challenges, group training experiences, and even financial-goal sites like the reddit frugality channel are so popular: people are more likely to engage in activities that require self-discipline when they are doing them with others.

Here's some data from MyFitnessPal to prove this point:

▲ Users who share their food diary with friends lose twice as much weight as other users do.

▲ Users who have ten or more friends lose, on average, four times as much weight as users who go it alone.

▲ Fifty-six percent of users said they prefer to exercise in some social context, because they get a better workout that way (65%), they work out harder with friends than they would on their own (50%) or they were flat-out more likely to show up and actually exercise than they would be alone (55%).[6]

I often saw this same sort of tribal HWW-goal pursuit with my real estate clients: no sooner would I start working with a couple on their lifestyle-design goals with home ownership than they would introduce me to two or three other friends who were trying to buy homes, too. This is the same phenomenon whereby Christopher's friend infected him, and he in turn infected his wife, with the get-fit bug; whereby Terese and her fellow moms kept each other on track with their cook-at-home goals; and whereby Giulia and her retreat colleagues helped each other do the follow-up work of manifesting their next career seasons.

One more thing: there can be a status component to social contagion around HWW goals. When I worked with Eventbrite some years back, we were always amazed at this truth: the most attended events were food and entertainment programs, but the ones people shared the most on social media were athletic-endurance events, runs, and races. Business and career-growth seminars came in a close second in events shared on social media. When we're spending our time and money in hot pursuit of self-improvement, we want others to know it!

Intersections: Their Journey and Yours

The brands mentioned in these hero's journeys have vanquished their own villains, the business killers of disengagement and distrust. And they have done much more than get people to click on a banner or watch their ads or make a one-time purchase. Their customers have fallen deeply, passionately, vocally in love with their offerings, content, and brands.

The companies that are engaging in these love affairs with their customers share a common commitment to removing resistance and inserting progress triggers along their customer-heroes' journeys to healthier, wealthier, wiser lives. These brands help prospective customers level up these areas of their lives—*whether or not they buy anything.* By doing so, they have become linchpins in the journeys of Transformational Consumers.

That's how *they've* done it. But a clear view of how your company can grow and thrive by serving Transformational Consumers can be seen only from a very particular intersection. That intersection is the spot where the Transformational Consumer's journey intersects with another journey line: yours.

CHAPTER FOUR

Your Call to Adventure

When a great ship is in harbor and moored, it is safe, there can be no doubt. But that is not what great ships are built for.

—DR. CLARISSA PINKOLA ESTÉS

TRANSFORMATIONAL TAKEAWAYS

1. Harnessing the force of human transformation to power a business is, itself, a Hero's Journey. Every Transformer business has one or more leader-heroes who consciously take it on that journey.
2. You are now being called to be a leader-hero in your company, regardless of your role, level, or function.
3. The stages of your Leader-Hero's Journey will require you to rethink what you sell, your customer, your marketing, your competition, and your team.

If you read business media at all, you are undoubtedly aware of the "list" awards and honors phenomenon: 100 Fastest Growing Companies, 75 Best Places to Work, Top 30 Executives under 30, and so forth.

One of these awards lists stands out among the rest: *Fast Company* magazine's Most Innovative Companies (MIC) list. This particular list is unique in that you can't apply to it. You can't game it. There's a real secret sauce to how it's put together. *Everyone* reads it. Some of the big guys make the list every year, like the FANG companies (Facebook, Apple, Netflix, Google). But they always make it for a kind of surprising reason or for a product line outside their core business that you don't really hear much about.

Every year, many companies make it to the list that you might never have heard of before. But you will definitely hear about them time and time again, once they hit the list.

MIC companies hold the cachet of having been officially deemed Fast Companies, with the paradoxical imprimatur of uber-cool innovation

54

coming out of fundamentally solid businesses. These companies are on the offense. They are winners.

The list is so respected and well read, at least in part, because the *Fast Company* editors and writers are some of the best business storytellers in the world. They have mastered the art of telling business stories, of telling the stories of the MIC companies, in a few different versions that differ in emphasis but all follow the Hero's-Journey model:

> **Version 1—The Customer Journey.** Millions of customers have an intractable problem. Leader of MIC Company has an insight into that problem and sets out on a mission to solve it. Leader and MIC Company create innovative solution. Millions of customers buy/use/love it.

> **Version 2—The Industry Journey.** Sector was dying, customers were fleeing or turning away. Leader of MIC Company starts using tool or strategy that has never been applied to this industry. Leader and MIC Company create innovative new offering(s). Millions of customers buy/use/love it.

> **Version 3—The Company Journey.** Company was floundering, failing, or even succeeding but in a "more of the same old" way. Leader of MIC Company has an insight about customer wants and needs and makes a surprising investment in company resources in something other than the core business. New offering(s) soar. Millions of customers buy/use/love it.

In every version of these MIC stories, the editors and writers generally configure their lengthier pieces to feature at least one company leader who was the champion of the changes that had to be made in order to get on the list. There is at least one leader, but often several, who played the hero's role in the transformational journey.

My question for you is this: are you willing to be that leader, to play that role, in your company?

Remember Why We're Here

Let's not forget why we're having this conversation in the first place. The whole reason we're here is that many of our companies are struggling with customer and employee disengagement, and that is severely limiting our ability to connect with customers and grow our businesses. We're not sure what they'll respond to and what they'll roll their eyes at.

We're having this conversation because another way is possible. A way of connection, customer engagement, employee engagement, and even love. To get there, we have to solve some concrete business problems that can be solved only by understanding our customers, strategically and systematically.

We know that if we engage our customers and our employees over and over again, we will succeed. Our companies will perform and soar. But it's unclear how to do that. We need direction and clarity. And then we'll need to change how we do what we do, to move in that direction, once we get it.

We have to be able to spot opportunities for innovating things our customers will love, buy, and use. We have to find junctures in their journeys for reconnection, for engaging them, and for developing loyalty, repeat business, and word-of-mouth referrals. And we have to know enough of the right things about them to lay the foundation for building beloved digital strategies, content programs, and brands: to transcend the transactional.

The Transformational Consumer Insights framework sketches out the landscape of human motivations on which we, as leaders, can begin to rebuild trust and engagement with our employees and our customers. But that's just the landscape, the context.

Now is where we take a beat and acknowledge one thing: that the modus operandi that got us here won't get us there. If we want to move beyond transactional relationships with our customers, we can't keep doing things the way we've been doing them. How much change we'll need to make is very case specific. For one company, there might need to be just some small but important "power tweaks" to our marketing messages. Another company may need to reorient almost every area of the business.

But in any event, unlocking growth and engagement by systematically harnessing the force of human transformation is a journey of its own. Consider the rest of this book as your personal guidebook for *that* journey.

The first stage of that journey is to rethink what you actually sell. In this stage, you'll be inspired to move out of that tired, old transactional belief system that you sell a product and into the inspired position that what you sell *is* a particular flavor and format of transformation.

The next stage of your company's journey to transcendence is to rethink your customer, redefining whom you serve through the lens of their journey and doing the research of actually talking and, more importantly, listening to real-life humans in your audience to create a set of key insights about their journey.

You will find this stage particularly powerful for reactivating checked-out employees. Have no fear—this stage does not necessarily require you to scrap your whole product line. After diving deep into your customers' journey, you will probably have some thoughts about product and service innovations. But you'll certainly be thinking about how to engineer an internal, whole-company mindset reset, as described by the Deloitte corporate learning adviser Josh Bersin:

> How do you create purpose, mission, and soul? Pharmaceutical companies are redefining themselves as wellness companies; retailers are redefining themselves as places for healthy food; tech companies define themselves as businesses to help people obtain information; and the list goes on. When you offer people a mission and purpose greater than financial return, you attract passionate individuals who want to contribute. And that brings a level of commitment and engagement no compensation package can create.[1]

The next several stages will require you to rethink your marketing, your metrics, and how you conceive of the competition. All of these stages help you translate your Transformational Consumer audience's real-life journeys into the elusive results we've already seen most companies so desperately lacking: customer engagement, loyalty, and love.

This point is critical: serving Transformational Consumers is not just about capturing more of a share of their wallets. It's about capturing a place in their hearts and their minds, which shows up in dozens of different, business-critical, quantifiable ways under a single header: engagement.

Think about this: the average person makes between 200 and 300 food-related decisions a day.[2] That's 300 moments related to food. The same goes for money-related decisions, career decisions, decisions about how people spend their time and their lives, small and large: thousands of decisions, all told, every day.

Using food as an example, it's obvious that no one buys food 300 times a day. But we think about food, choose something to eat, choose not to eat something, prepare food, go to the market, Google a recipe, pass up a food truck, grab a snack, make the kids a snack, order something on Instacart, make a dinner date, and the like 300 times every day.

And *many* of those 300 times will involve some level of contact with some brand, for better or for worse. Maybe it's making a reservation for a dinner a week out. Maybe it's as simple as reading a label or ripping into a food wrapper. Maybe it's reaching into the bag to put the groceries away or walking past a sign. Maybe it's reading a blog post or social media post online.

Every one of those times is not an opportunity to sell them something.

But many of those 300 daily food decisions *do* represent opportunities to connect and engage with that customer around food.

These nonspending engagements could go one of three ways: they could generate nothing, indifference. They could generate hate and disgust, such as the outrage that readers spewed at the brands in the *New York Times* article about the addictiveness of Cheetos.[3] Or they could generate love and respect and loyalty and word of mouth. The rest of this book is devoted to how to make this third scenario come to life for your company.

The most important tool you'll need is a team that is firing on all cylinders, engaged and in alignment with your new, transcendent vision, mission, and initiatives. The last stage of your journey involves rethinking your team to reorient them and poise them for this collective journey.

Your Call to Adventure

As with every good adventure story, the story of the Transformational Consumer has a plot twist. Like one of those films made up of vignettes with one or two intersecting characters or story lines, your Customer-Hero's Journey intersects with another fascinating story line: your journey as leader-hero.

There's an essential element of the hero's journey that I (intentionally) omitted to mention in chapter 3: the call to adventure. I didn't mention it explicitly up until now because everything you've read so far has, in fact, been a part of your own call to adventure.

Visualize yourself, right now, as you read this, as taking the first steps on a hero's journey of your own. Maybe the object of your quest is simply for your company to grow and thrive in any market climate. Or maybe your quest is actually a journey to self-actualization, to fulfilling your deepest purpose, to using your everyday work as a way to impact the world and solve the problems you desperately believe shouldn't plague the people you serve.

This is your call to the adventure of serving as the voice of the customer within your company, regardless of your title, regardless of your role. Whether you are the CEO of a public company, the sole proprietor of a local business, or a marketing director stuck in the middle level of a scaling start-up, hear me when I say that you can be a leader-hero, just like the ones featured in the MIC list.

If you are not (yet) an executive, I urge you to charge ahead anyway, keeping in mind that all transformation in companies happens from the inside out. Becoming one of several leader-heroes in the companies I've worked with was pivotal in honing my own purpose-driven, strategic voice and ultimately leveling up my career. Boldly taking up the mantle of reactivating and engaging customers through the lens of their HWW Aspirations was how I achieved the business results and developed the strategic voice, ultimately, that earned me a seat at the leadership table.

Consider yourself called.

And know, leader-hero, that where this journey, *your* journey, intersects with your Customer-Hero's Journey is where beloved businesses are built. Where brand love is born. Where products are innovated that change customers' behavior and bodies and bank accounts and even their businesses, for the better. Where content is created that people read and watch and love, because it changes people's lives for the better.

This is where businesses are tweaked and transformed in a way that takes the limits off what's possible for your career and your impact, your team, your company, and definitely your customer.

At the end of "The Extraordinary Science of Addictive Junk Food," Moss tells the story of the executive Jeffrey Dunn. Dunn's career path took him from running billions worth of Coke's North America business to using junk-food marketing strategies to sell carrots as the president and CEO of Bolthouse Farms (which has since been acquired by Campbell's).

Moss writes that when Dunn was called to brief Bolthouse investors on his plan for marketing carrots,

> "We act like a snack, not a vegetable," he told the investors. "We exploit the rules of junk food to fuel the baby-carrot conversation. We are pro-junk-food behavior but anti-junk-food establishment."
>
> The investors were thinking only about sales. They had already bought one of the two biggest farm producers of baby carrots in the country, and they'd hired Dunn to run the whole operation. Now, after his pitch, they were relieved. Dunn had figured out that using the industry's own marketing ploys would work better than anything else. He drew from the bag of tricks that he mastered in his 20 years at Coca-Cola, where he learned one of the most critical rules in processed food: The selling of food matters as much as the food itself.

As good business folk do, Dunn was also thinking of success. But, according to Moss, he was motivated by a desire to pay the world back for the harm he'd done by pushing sugary soda for years and years. Moss writes, "in his new line of work, Dunn told me he was doing penance for his Coca-Cola years. 'I'm paying my karmic debt,' he said."[4]

The other moral of Dunn's story is that you should not be daunted if you're not the head of R&D or the CEO or if you work in marketing or in HR or PR for that matter. When you decide to go into the business of behavior change, everything matters, not just the product. How you think about what you sell, how you market it, your understanding of customers and competition, and even your internal company culture: these, too, matter as much as the product itself.

These things might even matter more.

What got you here won't get you there. Rethinking things—rethinking everything—will.

CHAPTER FIVE

Rethink What You Sell

The best—maybe the only?—real, direct measure of "innovation" is change in human behaviour.

—STUART BUTTERFIELD

TRANSFORMATIONAL TAKEAWAYS

1. You sell a transformation, not a product.
2. Problem-First > product-first.
3. Use the story spine as a change-management tool to go from product-first to Problem-First.

Slack defines itself on its website by what it does. And what the company does, its stock-in-trade, is "bring all of a company's internal communications together in one place." At the next layer of detail, the company website specifies that the Slack app provides real-time messaging, archiving, and search for modern teams.

But internally, Slack's CEO, Stuart Butterfield, answered the question "What do we sell?" in an unexpected, impactful way. In an internal email he sent to all hands two weeks before launching the wildly popular Slack app, Butterfield asked his team to move past the idea that the company's product is group chat software:

> We are unlikely to be able to sell "a group chat system" very well: there are just not enough people shopping for group chat system (and, as pointed out elsewhere, our current fax machine works fine).
>
> What we are selling is not the software product—the set of all the features, in their specific implementation—because there are just not many buyers for this software product. (People buy "software" to address a need they already know they have or perform some specific task they need to perform, whether that is tracking sales contacts or editing video.)
>
> However, if we are selling "a reduction in the cost of communication" or "zero effort knowledge management" or "making better

decisions, faster" or "all your team communication, instantly search-able, available wherever you go" or "75% less email" or some other valuable result of adopting Slack, we will find many more buyers.

That's why what we're selling is organizational transformation. The software just happens to be the part we're able to build & ship (and the means for us to get our cut).

We're selling a reduction in information overload, relief from stress, and a new ability to extract the enormous value of hitherto useless corporate archives. We're selling better organizations, better teams. That's a good thing for people to buy and it is a much better thing for us to sell in the long run. We will be successful to the extent that we create better teams.[1]

Now, Slack is a B2B company. Its customers are teams and enterprises. So of course it makes sense that the transformation Butterfield initially focused on was organizational. But the decision makers who subscribe their companies and the team members who need to use it to be successful are each individual people, individual consumers. I'd hazard a guess that those to whom Slack appeals are more likely than not Transformational Consumers.

They are people who want to excel at their work, people who want to make the most of their work life so they can be more productive, be more fulfilled, be more efficient, earn more, create more, and ultimately have more time to spend with their families and pastimes. And at least in the early wave of adoption, which started here in Silicon Valley, they are likely people whose income, their actual compensation, is partly dependent on the company's success, via stock options.

If Butterfield asked me, I would say that Slack sells both organizational transformation and individual transformation, for the wealthier and the wiser.

A year after Butterfield sent this prelaunch email, Slack was live with over 60,000 teams and over 700,000 paid seats.[2] The app went from having 16,000 daily active users at launch in February 2014 to over 2.3 million daily active users in March 2016. The company has been valued at well over $3 billion. And Slack has been named by *Financial Times* as the first business technology to have crossed over into personal use since Microsoft Office and the Blackberry.[3]

What You Sell Is Transformation

Most companies think they sell a product. To transcend the transactional, your company must expand the way it conceives of what it sells. Like Slack, your company must sell a possibility: it must sell a specific sort of transformation, a specific sort of behavior change, a specific sort of journey from a problematic status quo to the new levels and possibilities that will unfurl after the behavior change you help make happen.

I understand that this is asking a lot, to challenge a whole company to change the very way it conceives of itself. Even if you buy the concept that Transformational Consumers are essential to your business, you might resist this admittedly massive paradigm shift. So, before I go into how to make this shift, let's talk about why you should make it.

The truth is that this is a shift that companies must make to survive whether or not they are interested in serving the Transformational Consumer. But if you know the Transformational Consumer is essential to your business, it's nonnegotiable.

Product-First or Problem-First

You really only have two choices. You can be a product-first company or a Problem-First company. There are companies that build things that they are good at building and then look to their marketing teams to get them sold. These are what I call product-first companies.

Other companies build things that people want or need to solve a real-life Problem they have. These are Problem-First companies.

Product-first is the descriptor I use for companies whose entire identity, R&D pipeline, offerings, marketing, and internal cultural narrative are oriented around a focus on *their products*, their features, their pricing, and what the products do—their function or even their benefit to the customer.

▲ The dictionary name of the product might actually be part of the company's name, whether it's paper, software, bikes, or shoes.

▲ The company's brand guidelines are rigid and unyielding, even in the face of evidence that its brand messages and communications are not effective with customers.

▲ The company's research program is the CEO taking things home and trying them out or a group of people charged with finding evidence to confirm the rightness of whatever the CEO has already decided to do.

▲ Product-first companies pride themselves on being very good at making their kind of product. They pride themselves on having great institutional knowledge of how to deliver the best versions of that product into the marketplace. They talk about themselves in terms of being the biggest, best, most innovative, or oldest producer of their type of product in the world.

Problem-First companies operate very differently. Sure, if you ask them what they sell, the literal answer might be a particular category of product. But Problem-First companies' point of view is a fixation on solving a Problem or set of problems for a particular customer audience or segment. They lead with that. They innovate by that. Their institutional knowledge is focused on knowing everything about the Problem they solve and the people who have that Problem. Their R&D program is a constant exploration of all the ways that this Problem could be mitigated at any given time, by their product or otherwise.

As our world grows ever more complex and the way customers interact with products changes, Problem-First companies are able to evolve in step with customers and with the market. They constantly evolve their offerings to meet consumers where they are and solve their Problem, however that Problem manifests itself at a given moment in time.

The Perils of Product-First

Don't get me wrong: you can *become* a successful company with a product-first mindset, so long as you find product-market fit at one moment in time.

Historically, product-first made total sense. When there were three paper vendors, it was super important to let people know (a) that you were one of them and (b) that your paper was better than the other companies' paper. As companies got larger and larger and needed a guiding principle around which to innovate, it became more important for them to focus and specialize.

Product-first made sense back then.

But in a sophisticated marketplace, with sophisticated buyers who have near-infinite products to choose from and a cacophonous media environment through which your marketing messages must break through, product-first simply no longer works for reaching and engaging customers.

What Transformational Consumers care about are *their* problems, *their* dreams, and *their* lives. The companies that are committed to alleviating those problems, facilitating those dreams, and improving those lives are the ones that Transformational Consumers pay attention to.

To be product-first is to be attached to *your* product, in your mind, in the minds of your employees, and in the minds of your customers—those you have and those you wish you could get through to. The best case scenario for a product-first company is that customers understand their product and why they need it, prefer it over competing products, and try it, hopefully more than once.

Unfortunately, there are many scenarios that are more common than the best case scenario. You might have experienced one or more of them:

▲ People don't understand your product.

▲ People don't understand why they need it.

▲ People prefer to buy a competing product.

▲ People try your product once but never again.

▲ Once-loyal customers eventually switch to a new product or switch to a totally new category of product.

If you are comfortable with your product being viewed by customers as a commodity, because you feel that your product always wins on price or quality, then being product-first and operating with a literal answer to the question of what you sell might be fine.

Until it's not.

If your product is so innovative that people might not actually know what it is or why they need it, product-first is not the approach to take.

If your product needs to constantly compete in the marketplace (and, trust me, *it does*), ditch product-first.

If you need people to buy your product over and over again—and you almost certainly do—product-first will only ever work for a season.

Here's why.

Product-First Companies Have a Limiting View of What They Do

If your self-concept as a company leads with product, that will limit how creative your product and marketing can ever be. If your self-concept as a company leads with a transformation you want to create, it empowers all of your teams to think much more broadly and creatively about ways you can facilitate that transformation.

This point was not lost on Butterfield, who wrote in his prelaunch email,

Consider the hypothetical Acme Saddle Company. They could just sell saddles, and if so, they'd probably be selling on the basis of things like the quality of the leather they use or the fancy adornments their saddles include; they could be selling on the range of styles and sizes available, or on durability, or on price.

Or, they could sell horseback riding. Being successful at selling horseback riding means they grow the market for their product while giving the perfect context for talking about their saddles. It lets them position themselves as the leader and affords them different kinds of marketing and promotion opportunities (e.g., sponsoring school programs to promote riding to kids, working on land conservation or trail maps). It lets them think big and potentially be big.[4]

Product-First Companies Build Products and Brand and Marketing Campaigns Based on This Limiting View of Why They Exist

Product-first companies build the things they know how to build and then look to their marketing teams to convince people to use them. The Problem is that people's minds and values and dreams aren't broken down into product categories—they want what they want, or what they think they want, on the basis of the real problems and challenges they face in their real lives.

Problem-First companies work to fix these problems *and* to translate their fix into customers' preexisting mental frames for things they already care about.

Product-first companies ask too much of their audiences. You're already asking them to change their behavior to buy your product and to use it and to buy it again. To also ask them to interpret your product into their personal value systems is simply too much to ask. People won't do it. More importantly, they don't have to—some other company is already out there doing a brilliant job of translating what they sell into terms that already mean something important to customers.

Product-First Companies May Succeed with an Initial, Innovative Product but Struggle to Innovate Competitively over the Long Run

Often, a product-first company's initial product was developed by a founder who was a member of the customer group, had the same Problem that customers in that group have, and innovated a solution to it. But if the company then begins to idolize that product, there will be neither direction nor impetus for innovation. It'll build years and years of new products that are slight tweaks on the old. You see it flailing and floundering to keep up with other, more innovative companies, because the DNA of innovation requires detachment and focus on a customer group and its Problem, not on the product itself.

Successful Product-First Companies Will Nearly Always Be Disrupted by Purpose-Driven, Behavior-Changing, Problem-First, People-First Companies

Hotels kept making slightly better hotels, while Airbnb innovated ways people could travel and live like locals. Taxi companies kept making new taxis, while Uber innovated ways people could use the newest human body part (their smartphone) to get their physical bodies and other items wherever they need them to be, on demand.

This will continue to happen: companies that fixate on solving a Problem will build subject-matter expertise around that Problem and, as a result, will disrupt the companies that fixate on their product.

This last point is a cautionary note for even the Ubers and Airbnbs of the world. Despite the fact that they are changing virtually every industry right now, many disruptive tech companies are actually product-first. I chalk this up to the fact that most tech-company founders and leaders are actually technical, product people—they are engineers and coders, by background. They love to play around with technology and built lots of things before finding one thing that found a product-market fit.

Most tech investors and venture capitalists are also fixated on technology, looking to put money into multiple products that use a certain technology in a gamble to find one that fits, versus seeking to deeply understand a Problem and a customer segment and then organizing their investments and innovations around that.

The other Problem with product-first in a tech environment is that you may innovate products way before people are ready for them, without being able to create the behavior change you need to succeed as a business. In Silicon Valley, it is often said that pioneers perish, but settlers prosper. In a TED talk, "The Surprising Habits of Original Thinkers," the Wharton professor Adam Grant said that about 47% of "first-mover" companies fail.[5] Often the first couple of innovative products in a category are *so* avant-garde that people have no idea they need them or struggle to create behavior change around using them regularly. It's only after a MySpace and a Yahoo! and widespread mobile-phone adoption, the thinking goes, that a Facebook can thrive. (Side note: RIP MySpace and Yahoo!.)

Pioneers *can* prosper. But historically, the only times they have is when they took a Problem-First approach; then rigorously, consistently created products that solved the Problem; *and then* marketed that product with constant reference to that Problem so that people would know the product is actually for them even though they've never heard of anything like it before.

This is what we call "making a market." It's hard to do but not impossible. Butterfield described it as "marketing from both ends" when he wrote to his team:

We should be working carefully from both the product end and the market end [by]:

▲ Doing a better and better job of providing what people want (whether they know it or not)

▲ Communicating the above more and more effectively (so that they know they want it).[6]

How to Become a Problem-First Company

There are two parts to every Problem-First mindset: you must know *the Problem* your company exists to solve, and you must understand *the people* who have that problem.

Don't think because I'm using the term "Problem" that your customer must be experiencing a dysfunction or disorder, breakdown, or crisis. The capital P "Problem" of your company's Transformational Consumer audience simply refers to the specific Personal Disruption Conundrum that they are experiencing and that your company can help solve. The Problem is the specific behavior change they want to make. It's the specific health, wealth, or wisdom goal they hope to reach, with your help.

TRANSFORMER CASE STUDY IN HELPING PEOPLE "DO" THEIR DREAMS: PLATFORMS THAT TRANSFORM

Google Goals

While I was writing this book, Google released a feature called, simply, Goals. This capability of the company's billion-user Calendar software allows people to block time off for Goals versus just for events. But it's more robust than just that: once a customer sets up a Goal, such as make a budget, and until that goal is marked "finished," the Google Goals algorithm will actively search for unbooked time slots that seem opportune for working on the Goal and suggest them to the user.[7]

Rich Pins

The Google feature announcement reminded me of something I'd heard Pinterest was working on: "rich pins" that brands can use to help Pinners take action on the content they pin. I rang up my friend Christine Weil Schirmer, Pinterest's head of communications. "Our mission is actually to help people discover and do the things they love. Rich pins are one feature we have built that is an example of how we do that. We know the value of the ideas people are pinning is in people being able to actually complete them and improve their lives."

There are five categories of rich pins, which are essentially content pins that are more robust than normal. For example, Schirmer explained,

> For the category of food, we have a rich pin we call the recipe pin. It takes the information from the recipe webpage being pinned and pulls out the ingredients, preparation, and cooking time onto the pin itself, so people can see it at a glance. We also just launched something we call 'How To' cards, which are rich pins that pull out step-by-step instructions from the content a Pinner is adding to their board, making it more likely that they'll actually complete the project.

> The reason why these products have been developed is that we know 80% of our users are pinning to our platform, this great, global catalogue of ideas, from mobile devices. Rich pins are our way of surfacing the critical information they need to make those ideas and dreams actionable.[8]

The Transformational Subreddits

There's one more Transformational Consumer platform that might surprise you: reddit. The site is known for its religious adherence to principles of free speech and minimal facilitation, which have allowed some very dark communities and conversations to take root on the site. Less well-known are reddit's more rigorously moderated Transformational Consumer communities, which flourish on "subreddit" communities, like r/personalfinance, r/fitness, r/frugal, and r/minimalism.

▲ These subreddits serve as a friendly, if uncensored, space online where Transformational Consumer tribes connect to encourage each other, ask questions, and share knowledge.

▲ They facilitate personal development in health, wealth, wisdom areas on a single portal: reddit.

▲ reddit's staunch dogmatic agnosticism as a platform promotes diverse opinions and robust discussions, so many sides of an issue get voiced.

▲ AMAs: reddit's "Ask me anything" franchise allows Transformational Consumers on these particular subreddits to connect directly with HWW influencers and get answers to their personal questions.

▲ Recurring weekly threads and "editorial franchises" hold space for the predictable, subject-specific content and inspiration cravings of Transformational Consumers. All of these subreddits feature evergreen, beginner knowledge on transformational topics in "Start here" or "FAQ" channels.

For example, with over six million subscribers, the r/fitness subreddit community home page has a "Getting Started" wiki with sections for "defining your goals," "fixing your diet," and "starting exercise."

This subreddit also runs a well-established weekly calendar of recurring features: Victory Sunday, Moronic Monday, Training Tuesdays, Rant Wednesdays, Nutrition Thursdays, Physique Phridays (also Foolish Fridays), Self-Promotion Saturdays, and Gym Story Saturdays, too.[9]

Use the Story Spine to Rethink What You Sell and Shift to Problem-First

The power of anecdote is so great that it has a momentum in and of itself. No matter how boring the facts are, you feel inherently as if you are on a train that has a destination.

—IRA GLASS

One tool I've used to help companies understand how to orient around their own Transformational Consumer and that customer's behavior-change Problem is something I learned from the world of improv, of all places.

It's called a story spine. For my dime, it is the fastest, most effective tool I've ever used to work with leaders through the process of rethinking what they sell.

The story spine is a simple template for telling a story, and it goes like this:

1. Once upon a time, there was ___.
2. Every day, ___.
3. Until one day, ___.
4. And because of that, ___.
5. And because of that, ___.
6. And because of that, ___.
7. Until finally, ___.
8. And ever since then, ___.

Fill in the first blank with your customer. Fill in the second blank with the Problem your customer is experiencing: the behavior or status quo about your customer's life that he or she wants to change.

Now—and this is critical—do not, for the love of all that is sacred, fill in blank 3 with some version of "they used MagicGlo toothpaste" or whatever your product is. Trust me—you will be tempted to do this. Fight this temptation. Most companies at least have an answer for what they sell. They have an elevator pitch for their product, a tagline, SKUs, maybe even a set of statements like vision, mission, purpose, and such, that they trot out in answer to that question.

But this doesn't actually work. Not if you want to reach and engage Transformational Consumers, which I'll assume you do, since you've read this far.

Blank 3 must be filled in with some progress or behavior-change trigger. Blanks 4–6 are for the behavior change and the consequences thereof. And blank 7 is for the "Aspiration achieved" state of the customer's life.

Where is your product in this story spine? Most often, when it's done right, it's implied. Again, what Transformer companies sell—what you sell, if your company wants to be one—is not a product.

What You Sell Is the Transformation Itself

You sell a particular category of behavior change and its consequences. What you sell is the transformation, the behavior change that happened that one day, to go back to the story spine. And you also sell everything that changed about the protagonist's life as a result of that change, all of the "because of thats," the "until finally," and the "and ever since then."

Here are some considerations that will help you create your company's story spine:

▲ **Tell the story of your Customer-Hero's Journey.** Remember, in the archetypal Hero's Journey as we apply it to Transformational Consumers, your company plays the role of mentor, adviser, guide, tool (or supply) to the customer-heroes you serve. If you create a story spine, you might want to keep the specifics of how your product helps the customer relatively vague, directional, or implied. This helps keep it open as to specifically how your brand and company will empower and aid the people you serve.

▲ **Your customer matters most, but your beliefs, theory of change, and values matter, too.** The story spine can hold the space not only for the Problem and the people you serve but also for your values, beliefs, and the wrongs in the world that your company hopes to right. With intentionally selected words, it can paint a picture of how you believe change will happen and what function you want to fulfill, in your Customer-Hero's Journey, without overprescribing or overemphasizing your company, distracting focus from your customer.

Remember B. J. Fogg's Functional Triad and the other progress triggers—they can also inspire how your company shows up in the story spine. Experiment with ways your story might answer these questions, when it comes to the role your company or your products play:

- Do you facilitate or simplify what's hard on your customers' journeys with knowledge or logistical ease?
- Do you remove resistance? How?
- Do you hope to provide tools that make something hard easier or to lead your customers through a process?
- What triggers your customers to make change?
- Do people see others model their ideal behavior or get social support or encouragement?

▲ **Use the story to make your shift from product-first to Problem-First stick.** The power of the story spine to help reorient your team members is driven by the power of narrative. Unlike many other ways you can communicate a message throughout your company, this story will stick with them.

The goal of this exercise is not only to rethink your actual product and what you sell. It's also to rethink the prioritization your whole organization places on product versus Problem, especially if it has been fetishizing the product itself since time immemorial. The Problem and the people who have it, your customers, move to priority one. Product comes after.

▲ **There's no perfect, final story spine.** There's no just-right answer for how this comes out. The story spine is just the very first step of shifting your company's orientation from product-first to Problem-First. But it's a powerful first step and can be especially helpful in activating others to see your vision for this shift and to begin a change-management action plan in this direction.

So use the story spine to kick this process off. But see it as an organic, evolving project—a constant work in process. Hone and revise it as you work through the rest of the questions and shifts recommended throughout this book, as you rethink your customer, your marketing, your competition, and your company culture.

Many Teams, One Single Story

By the time you're on the final rethink of your Leader-Hero's Journey, you'll be able to use the story spine as a check and balance, even a decision rubric, that every single person in the company can use. If a new product feature or marketing campaign does not fall in line with this narrative or does not further the transformation story of your hero-customer, that's a great signal to revisit the thinking and decision making behind the initiative, before it gets too far gone.

This is not a matter of just marketing or messaging or semantics. If you do it right, your Problem-First approach will permeate everything about overall company strategy, research and development, product-market fit, design, customer service, *and then also* content and marketing.

Now, to make this all concrete, here's an example of a story spine I developed a few years back with my clients at Lumo Body Tech.

The Lumo Body Tech Story Spine

Once upon a time, there was a man, woman, athlete, or desk jockey. In fact, there were tens of millions of them. And every day, they sat too much and moved too little, slouching on the couch, in the car, or at the computer.

Until one day, they had developed bad posture.

And because of that, they had back pain, looked less attractive, became less active, and lost confidence.

And because of that, they took pills, had surgery, and made all sorts of (unsuccessful) efforts to fix their posture.

And because of that, they got depressed, experienced side effects, and ultimately lost some of the joy of living.

Until one day, they started tracking their posture and setting small movement goals.

And since then, they stood up more, sat less, moved more, and developed correct posture. And so they looked better/thinner/hotter, their backs were pain-free, and they were healthier and more active. They burned more calories. And so they felt alive and more powerful and were able to fulfill their potential in life and at work.

Postscript: And now they also know how to achieve any health goal or change any habit they want.

Problem-First = Purpose-Driven = Profitable

My friend and mentor Jim Stengel was the global CMO for Proctor and Gamble for years. During his tenure, he managed over 7,000 employees and a multibillion-dollar annual marketing budget, reviving brands like Covergirl and Pampers with what he calls a "purpose-driven" approach to brand management.

RETHINK YOUR BUSINESS MODEL

Transformer Case Study: Credit Karma
(Aspiration: Wealthy and Wise)

Credit Karma's 50 million members have used the platform to access more than one billion of their own credit scores since 2007. The staffer Frances Cohen told me that the company defines itself as "a platform that helps make financial progress possible for everyone."[10]

Credit Karma's defining what it sells as "financial progress" is by no means a given, in a field of companies that get paid by banks for every consumer lead or every consumer click. The company's model is to never charge consumers and to only take a fee from its bank partners when customers successfully receive the credit they apply for. The company calls this its win-win-win model, a legacy of Credit Karma's launch in 2007, at the peak of consumer distrust of and disgust with the financial markets.

Sixty million Credit Karma customers use the site's score access and dispute features to raise their credit score, which translates into interest-rate savings. Providing clear insight into the murky world of debt and credit scores and empowering members to save money by improving their scores at no cost? That's progress.

Stengel teaches that a brand's purpose is a living, breathing organism rooted in ideals. The deepest roots are the people your company serves. Out of these roots grows what Stengel calls the brand ideal, "a shared goal of improving people's lives." He goes on, "A brand ideal is a business's essential reason for being, the higher-order benefit it brings to the world." He shares a valuable model for building purpose into every element of the business in his book *Grow: How Ideals Power Growth and Profit at the World's Greatest Companies* (2011).

Stengel teamed up with the research firm Millward Brown and analyzed the performance of over 50,000 companies across a ten-year period of time, comparing companies on the basis of whether they were product-first or Problem-First (i.e., purpose-driven). Here are the results:

▲ The 50 top-performing companies were brands built on a differentiated statement of higher human ideals, a purpose statement similar to what we're calling the "Problem-First" approach here.

▲ These companies' stock price grew three to four times faster than their competitors' did.[11]

So how is "purpose" different from "Problem," as I'm using it here? It's not. Jim once told me that his definition of "brand" includes, well, everything—he defines "brand" as the collective behavior of everyone at your company. By design, then, that would include product design, engineering, customer service, and research and development.

That said, my experience teaches that all employees might not internalize this broad a definition of "brand" or "purpose." When most people hear "purpose," they think marketing, corporate social responsibility, or maybe branding. There's a connotation that purpose is a snap-on marketing message that can be built on top of an otherwise product-first company.

So I stay away from the term "purpose" when advising companies on the change-management process away from product-first, because employees' existing mental categories often slot "purpose" under brand, marketing, or generally "something I don't have to think about if I don't work in marketing."

On the other hand, the word "Problem" conjures up something that is desperately waiting to be fixed. And *that* causes even the most marketing-detached product engineer or user-experience designer to prick up his or her ears and get interested in creating solutions.

In fact, Stengel's framework for disseminating purpose throughout a company includes "delivering a near-ideal customer experience," an aim that necessarily includes delivering a product that enchants and delights the people who buy and use it.[12] Marketing alone won't get it. Butterfield echoed this mandate in his prelaunch email, writing, "we need to do an exceptional, near-perfect job of execution" in order to get people to try a product they don't even know they need yet.[13]

Manifesto Marketing

"People don't buy what you sell; they buy why you sell it," says Simon Sinek, the TED star and author of *Start with Why*.[14] Manifesto marketing makes the most of this truth, attracting a tribe of people who agree whether or not they happen to be in the market for the company's product at a particular moment in time.

I call it manifesto marketing when a company broadcasts the reasons *why* it does what it does, its values, or its beliefs externally, even if they are not strictly related to its products, incorporating them in its communications, products, or packaging.

The best known example of manifesto marketing is the lululemon manifesto, a long list of declarations of the company's beliefs about how to live a long, healthy life, which is emblazoned on the company's signature red-and-white reusable bags and even on some of its actual products.

But manifesto marketing may include executive thought leadership on topics that are more tangentially related to the business, such as Sheryl Sandberg's new-classic book *Lean In*[15] and Arianna Huffington's *Thrive*.[16] And open letters on subjects that are only distantly related to what the company sells also qualify, such as the "welcome to the world" letter that Mark Zuckerberg published when his daughter was born.[17]

Even internal communications can serve as manifesto marketing, if they get out. One of the most visible examples in recent history was Zuckerberg's email detailing his and the company's support of the Black Lives Matter movement after the motto was replaced with "All Lives Matter" on a board at the company HQ.[18]

Manifestos are less about what you sell and more about why and how you sell it, how you operate, or how you see the world. But the why, how, and worldview are like magnets to your company's tribe of Transformational Consumers, inspiring them to take action and connect with your brand.

TRANSFORMER CASE STUDY: TARGET

Target didn't just declare a commitment to furthering customers' health and wellness goals in 2015. The retailer made a series of massive strategic and marketing moves to make it easier for everyday Transformational Consumers to find and afford the wellness-promoting products right where they already are, at Target, in the food section and at the checkout counter.

Rather than plopping a health-washed veneer on top of business as usual, Target spent 2015 rolling out a robust, holistic program of initiatives and power moves to remove all sorts of frictions along the health journeys of *both* their internal and external audiences:

February 2015: Doubled the number of organic, natural, and sustainable brands it promotes under the Made to Matter umbrella. Target's Made to Matter collaborations drive mainstream discovery of now hundreds of healthier baby, beauty and personal care, grocery, health-care, and household products, in partnership with such brands as Annie's Organics, Burt's Bees, and Horizon Organic.

May 2015: Convened a meeting of a handful of Big Food brands—including Kellogg's, General Mills, and Campbell's Soup—at its Minneapolis headquarters to preview the next generation of the grocery section: less space for processed, much more space for produce and healthful, fresh foods. Target used the occasion to advise these processed-food brands that they should either create new, healthier products or expect to lose shelf space.

Food products that fall under "wellness" would get the retailer's promotional support and in-store real estate going forward, Target warned suppliers. Those that don't would not.

"That doesn't mean that mac and cheese is being eliminated, but clearly assortment is being shaped around what consumers are looking for," Target CEO's, Brian Cornell, told the press at the time.[19]

That same month, Target announced a reorganization of each store's product assortment into a handful of categories, including wellness, which covers portions of both packaged and fresh foods, apparel, and pharmacy segments of the stores. This move was unprecedented among retailers of Target's scale, positioning the new, hybrid "wellness" category as one of the chain's three high-priority, fast-growth segments.[20]

June 2015: Announced partnership with CVS in Target pharmacies in about 1,660 stores nationwide, including plans for the brands to join forces on customizing health and wellness pharmacy offerings in these stores-within-a-store to local customers' wellness wants and needs.[21]

September 2015: Doubled down on wellness, announcing an experiment in which 30 Target stores would swap out junk and sugary foods at the checkout counter with healthier options, like KIND bars. Simultaneously became Fitbit's largest corporate customer, providing 300,000 employees with fitness trackers for their own use—not to be monitored by Target corporate.[22]

"There's both a huge business opportunity here and a bit of a moral imperative," Christina Hennington, SVP of merchandising for Target, told the press at the time. "Our ultimate goal is to improve the health of the nation."[23]

January 2016: Launched Target x SoulCycle partnership, which brought cobranded merchandise and a series of pop-up indoor cycling studios, complimentary classes, and weekend experiences to ten cities around the nation just in time for New Year's resolutions.[24]

Target sells a lot of things. But it transcends the transactional by staying clear that one of the most important things it sells is wellness. In the process, it has shifted its focus to resolving the frictions its customers face as they try to live well. "We know our guests care about wellness and are focused on making better choices for themselves, their families and communities," said Laysha Ward, chief corporate social responsibility officer for Target. "Plus, for the first time in centuries, our children are expected to have shorter life expectancies than we are. Through this shift in strategy, we want to improve the health of the nation by making wellness the way of life."[25]

CHAPTER SIX

Rethink Your Customer

TRANSFORMATIONAL TAKEAWAYS

1. Your customers are not just the people in your existing customer base. Your customer is anyone and everyone trying to solve the Personal Disruption Conundrum, achieve the goal, or engage in the healthy, wealthy, or wise lifestyle that you help with or support.
2. Deeply, accurately understand these people's real-life journeys, with both quantitative and qualitative research, validating with data along the way.
3. Align every team, every product, and every initiative in your company around the same understanding of your customers' journeys.

You don't sell a product. You sell a transformation, a journey from one point to another—a journey from having a problem to being free of it.

Rethinking your customer follows naturally. "Your customer" is not just the people who literally already have or use your product. Your customer is everyone who has the problem that your company exists to serve.

Understanding your customers' journey, the problem, and their real-life experience trying to solve it—that's what it takes to rethink your customer.

From: Your existing customer base, user base, or social media followers.

To: Everyone who has the human-scale, high-level Problem your company exists to solve.

TRANSFORMER CASE STUDY: MyFitnessPal

When I first came to MyFitnessPal as a consultant, the company had tens of millions of users, and no marketing team. It was a testament to the magnetic force of a simple product that works to fix a big behavior-change problem that a whole lot of people

---

have. One of the first things I wanted to know was what the company knew about the Personal Disruption Conundrum that most of its users were downloading the app to solve: weight loss.

Now, I had a lot of solid guesses about what the experience of trying to lose weight looks like, in real life. I had a base of solid factual knowledge in this realm; I had been working with Transformational Consumer brands for years, at that point. And I myself had lost 60 pounds almost 20 years earlier. But I also knew that I couldn't be the representative of every weight-concerned human being in the world.

So I dug around. And it turned out that the only research the company had done to that point was some interviews and panels of a few handfuls of its existing San Francisco users.

This waved two big red flags:

Issue 1: These people had already downloaded the app. If I was going to build a marketing program to grow our engaged user base, I needed to know about the people who hadn't already gotten the app—*especially* people who had never heard of our app!

Issue 2: The second glaring issue was this: San Francisco. *San Francisco.* I mean, I love the Bay Area more than just about anyone and have lived here for 20 years myself. But in no way are San Franciscans representative of any class of humanity anywhere else on the planet—not with respect to what they eat and certainly not when it comes to how they use technology.

We needed to rethink our customers. So we did. And what we found allowed us to transcend a strictly transactional relationship with our customers, driving a steep, sustained uptick in how often we engaged with our customers via product features and content, fast.

But first, we had to stop thinking of our customers as the people who were already using our product.

The critical group of people we needed to understand was everyone in the world who was trying to solve this problem.

Then, we had to get out of our office and into the real world, into our customers' world—or, more accurately, their worlds, plural. We couldn't just ask them a bunch of outright questions. We needed to see their actual behavior and actual surroundings.

We had to rethink what their journeys even meant. We needed to shift from focusing solely on their life cycle using our product to deeply understanding their real-life journeys of trying to change their behavior.

Ultimately, we kicked off a customer research project that spanned nearly two years and multiple continents before it was done. The insights we gleaned drove the growth of our engaged user base by over 200% just in the first year of the project.

One reason the insights were so powerful was that, early on, we invested a great deal of thought into how we defined the Problem. We decided to ask ourselves a much bigger, much more important question than "How do people experience the weight-loss journey?" We asked this question instead: "What does the journey from unhealthy to healthier look like?"

And we invested a great deal at the other end of the project, too. We carefully crafted outputs of the research and then indoctrinated the whole company in the results, intensively, for many months. This empowered every single team in the company to operate from this singular customer journey model.

It worked for us. And it continues to work for the brands the TCI team helps deconstruct, model, and immerse in their customers' journeys. Here's some insight into the power and process of customer journey mapping, the way we see it and run it.

How to Translate Your Customers' Lives into a Usable Journey Map

The first thing we did, at MyFitnessPal, was get out of town. We put together a list of six cities that represented the various points of view and lifestyles other than the coastal, urban, techie, early adopter audience viewpoints we had already captured in San Francisco. We recruited an intentionally diverse assortment of research subjects in those towns from among a large set of people who said yes when we asked the qualifying question, "Are you trying to live a healthier life than you do now?"

Sometimes we asked people straightforward questions. But rule number one of humanity is that people don't always even know the truth of why they do what they do, even if they think they do. So other times, we used methods from psychology and the other behavioral sciences to get into their deeper, less conscious emotions and thoughts about the subject matter.

Still other times, we observed people, naturalistically. We went out and met them, in their own homes and their own gyms. We went into their refrigerators, their pantries, their spreadsheets, and occasionally, their phones.

We spent hours with each of them, learning about what healthy meant to them and letting them brief us on every kind of tool, support, and strategy they were using to try to change their behavior and change their lives. We explored what got them started on the path to healthy living, what got them stuck along the way, and what circumstances and mindsets moved them forward. We learned about who and what influenced them, for the healthier and for the worse.

We met with churchgoing moms on Herbalife and Crossfitting Chicagoans and all sorts in between. We met with people struggling with obesity and with others who'd achieved what we came to call the "effortful ease" of living a lifestyle that was more healthy than not, on net. We met with people in their 20s, 30s, 40s, and way beyond, at all levels of self-described health.

We recorded these interviews and documented them extensively with photos and transcripts.

We slowly began to spot patterns across all of these prospective customers' journeys from healthy to unhealthy, breaking them down into a series of stages that virtually everyone went through.

I can't share all the specifics of the process, nor can I divulge the entire journey model map we created: it's proprietary. The truth is that there's no single, right way to do these projects—what will be of high value to a given company and its initiatives will vary.

But I can share some of the things we were looking for then and the things we almost always look for in our research work at TCI now. These are the six things to make sure you look for as you rethink your customers by understanding their journey:

1. Universal Stages in the Journey

In almost every case, you will find that there is a sequence of events, mindsets, and experiences that people tend to share in common as they go from having the problem that your company exists to solve to success with that particular behavior change, Personal Disruption Conundrum, or goal. A very important objective of rethinking your customer should be to identify the stages of that journey and create a clear, visual model or map of it.

To be clear, I am not talking about customer journeys the way many companies use them: as a chart of the various touch points that a paying customer or existing user will have with the brand as they use the product. You may need a model of your customer's life cycle *with your product* in order to address disengagement and to reactivate your customers, but that's not what I'm talking about here.

When you're building the kind of Transformational Consumer customer journey map that I'm talking about, the end goal is to transcend the transactional. So *transcend the transactional*. Zoom way out, to a level much higher than your customers' experience with your product. Create a journey map that lays out their real-world, real-life experience of trying to go from unhealthy to healthy. Or from broke to debt-free. Or from stuck in a dead-end job to the next level of their career. Or from frustrated dreamer to successful small-business owner. Or from grappling with a certain set of physical symptoms to pain-free and in control of their bodies.

Zoom out. You can zoom back in later. The zoomed-in part—the life cycle with your product part—is much easier, more accessible, and probably more intuitive for your team to map out, if they haven't already. That part will get done.

2. Feelings and Behaviors

How do people feel, and what do people do at the various stages of the journey?

Also, what behavior-change levers do they try to pull? In weight loss, for example, there are generally two levers people try to pull to control their behavior: food and exercise. Eat less (or eat better) and exercise more.

Within each of those, there is a core set of changes that people try to make in order to make this happen. They try to cook or eat at home more. They might try to eat less processed and more whole foods. They track their calories or their food more generally. They join a gym or sign up for group exercise classes like Zumba or Crossfit. Each of these can be drilled down even further: to get to class, they might pack their gym bag the night before. To cook, they might create a written meal plan for the week.

This is a tiny sampling of all the levers people try to pull to lose weight, which is itself just one lever/subset of the "live a healthier life" goal. But as you can see, doing an inventory of the levers your customers naturally try to pull, in their real-world lives, to create the behavior change they want and need empowers you and your teams to make smart, strategic decisions about how you can help them and how you can't.

First, it helps to make it clear what levers don't work or bear too little fruit for the trouble it takes to move them. Second, it may illuminate opportunities for you to help create content or product features that move the needle a lot on a lever that people are generally struggling with. Third, it segues you to the natural next question: where do people get stuck or get unstuck on pulling these levers? The answers reveal some of the most fertile ground for product and content that changes behavior and repositions your brand.

3. Progress Triggers

What are all the things, in the real world (not just in your product line), that help people move successfully from one stage of their transformational journey to the next? You need an inventory of these things, too. Trust me, if you sit down with real people who have legitimately been trying to deal with a well-defined behavior-change objective, they will delightedly share the things that have moved them forward on the path.

For example, we learned a few general things about people who had previously been relatively inert and uninterested in taking action on their health:

▲ They were galvanized when a friend or relative successfully lost a lot of weight.

▲ They were activated when they saw a picture of themselves or caught an unflattering glance in the mirror.

▲ They were inspired to get into shape for an upcoming wedding or reunion.

▲ They were prompted into action by having recently given birth or gotten divorced.

Another big progress trigger, when it comes to weight loss, turned out to be actual progress, or momentum—once people actually saw a little movement on the scale, they were much more likely to stay in motion.

Medical diagnoses turned out to be less common triggers than we thought. But the realization that you are huffing and puffing after running a block, playing with your kid, or climbing a flight of stairs? Much more common than we expected.

Remember, people are not always rational. Often things people *think* will change their own behavior don't actually do so, which is part of why they are coming to brands and products for help. The power of customer research is that it reveals what organically causes change and what doesn't. And once you know that, you're in a position to double down on what works and stop investing in what doesn't.

4. Resistance: Obstacles, Quit Points, Rules of Thumb, and Decision Traps

Where do people get hung up? What gets them stuck? What common circumstances lead people to quit even trying? Where do they make decision shortcuts? What rules of thumb do they use, for better or for worse? The answers to each of these questions will reveal a deep set of topics for your editorial calendar.

When I worked with HGTV, ING Direct, and ultimately, Trulia, we used insights from my time in the car with hundreds of home buyers to surface that people often started house hunting online using a price range to their budget maximum, without appreciating that homes were selling for quite a lot above their asking prices. Once they had loved—and lost—multiple properties, people were often willing to break the bank and throw money at the next listing they liked, overspending and taking on unsustainable mortgage arrangements to make it happen. (You might have heard something about how this whole thing turned out. They called it the "Great Recession.")

Here's another example: during the MyFitnessPal ethnography, we flat-out asked people what their biggest obstacle to living a healthy life was. I'm not suggesting that overtly asking people questions and taking their answers at face value is always the right strategy. Again, they don't always actually even know the truth. But it can be very revealing, occasionally. And it was, on this occasion: almost to a person, our customers said their biggest obstacle to living a healthy life was budget. Healthy food costs a lot.

What's an app company supposed to do with that? Never in the history of the company had we heard that budget was a blocker to health. In San Francisco, it's nothing to spend $25 on a salad at lunch, so our local users were probably just not experiencing budget as a blocker the way people were everywhere else. We hypothesized that maybe it was just a perception issue. Maybe people were assuming they had to pick between Cheetos and grass-fed bison. Or maybe people just perceived eating burgers are cheaper than cooking because they'd never actually done the math.

So we asked a lot of follow-up questions. And we kept hearing people talk about these fast-food dollar menus. To be totally honest, at the risk of giving away the food snobbery of our team, we had no idea that virtually every fast-food chain in the country actually has a one-dollar-an-item menu. McDonald's has one—that, we knew. But so does Burger King, Taco Bell. The Fresco menu we kept hearing about was Taco Bell's dollar menu.

Even der Weinerschnitzel! One woman told us how her husband put himself on a five-dollar dinner budget, which meant five chili cheese dogs.

The math from there was simple: 320 calories and 16 grams of fat each equaled 1,600 calories and 80 grams of fat, more than he was supposed to eat in a day.

The even more stunning revelation, to us, was that a mother of four could feed her family 20 items of hot food for 20 dollars, without cooking—heck, *without even getting out of the car.*

We took a step back. This was a real issue. We took the view that everything that got between our customers and living a healthy lifestyle was potentially our competition. So we spent some time as a company exploring what we could possibly do to address this issue. The options were more numerous than you might think:

▲ We could help people find and fix food faster and cheaper, with recipe content that would be fast and inexpensive to cook.

▲ We could create content to help people budget and plan their meals in a way that helped level the playing field between healthy and unhealthy foods, from a cost and convenience perspective.

▲ We could seek out partnerships with healthy fast- and convenience-food brands, to get discounts for our customers.

▲ We could even exert pressure on the many fast-food chains that wanted to be our promotional partners to make healthy menu options more available or affordable.

Ultimately, we did end up doing some of these things, on the basis of a wide array of strategic inputs. The point here is that the exercise of understanding and inventorying the places our customers get stuck allowed us to systematically innovate solutions and then pick those that aligned well with our business model, strategic priorities for that time frame, resources, and core competencies.

5. Micro-Moments

As you inventory the stages of the journey and the things that get people stuck or unstuck along the way, you'll hear from the horses' mouths exactly where your customers go at different spots along their journey. By "where," I mean both physical and digital "locations." Some might be obvious, others less so. The power of the micro-moment is not just in knowing where customers go when they need knowledge—it's knowing where they go *at specific moments* in their journey. This is often much less obvious or intuitive and can reveal highly actionable insights, especially for your marketing efforts.

Originally, Google broke micro-moments down into the following buckets:

▲ I want-to-know moments

▲ I want-to-go moments

▲ I want-to-do moments

▲ I want-to-buy moments[1]

But as the framework has evolved, Google's consumer insights team spotted some patterns I would deem transformational micro-moments. These are patterns in how consumers use their mobile devices to do research projects related to their HWW goals. Google breaks them down and labels them in accordance with the findings of its consumer research:

▲ **Show-me-how moments.** These moments allow for brands to connect with customers who have already bought their products but are looking to know how to use them, creating opportunities for engagement, love, and referrals.

▲ **One-step-at-a-time moments.** Google found that "90% of smartphone users have used their phone to make progress toward a long term goal or multi-step process [like home buying] while 'out and about.'"

▲ **Time-for-a-change moments.** In introducing this transformational micro-moment category, the Google team profiled a young man whose bad day at work kicked off Internet research for graduate educational options and "snackable content" to "keep the dream alive."

▲ **New-day, new-me moments.** The Google team's conclusion that many "people try new things in routine moments" was based on its research finding that "91% of smartphone users turn to their phone for ideas while doing a given task."[2]

Pharma companies, for example, devote much of their marketing spending to physicians' offices. By doing so, they miss the many billions of online "I want to know" micro-moments of Transformational Consumers who may spend many months searching the Internet trying to diagnose their symptoms and look for home remedies before they ever even think about emailing or calling their doctor.

Here are a few data points from Google's micro-moments research:

▲ 91% of people do research and look up information on their phones while they're in the middle of another task.

▲ 82% of people go to the store to buy something and then consult their phones while they're trying to decide which thing to buy.

▲ 10% of these so-called showroomers buy a different product than originally planned.[3]

If you understand where along your customers' journey they experience "I want to know," "I want to go," and "I want to do" moments relevant to the problem you exist to solve, you can be there. And you can be there with content that serves what they want to do then, positioning yourself as the transformational partner they will undoubtedly go to when they are ready to buy.

6. Natural Language and Mental Frames

The value of your customers' natural language is threefold (at least):

▲ Your customers' natural language reveals how they frame the problem your business exists to solve in their minds, which could be very different from how you've been thinking about it.

▲ Understanding their mental frames empowers you to phrase your marketing and communications in the same terms your customers already use. It allows you to create content that gets their attention because it uses words they've already flagged as "Things I Care About."

This is what Stuart Butterfield meant when he told his team, "Just as much as our job is to build something genuinely useful, something which really does make people's working lives simpler, more pleasant and more productive, our job is also to understand what people think they want and then translate the value of Slack into their terms."[4]

▲ Content that addresses the obstacles and sticking points that your customers keep running into in their natural language builds credibility with your customers that you *get* them. That credibility boosts the chances that Transformational Consumers will give your product a try, too.

At MyFitnessPal, one of the most powerful outcomes of the customer research project was a set of message pillars we used to build a wildly popular content program. We got to ten million unique visitors monthly in about a nine-month period of time by strategically publishing content across our email newsletter, blog, social media, and in-app content program. All of the content solved customer problems that we spotted and promoted progress triggers from the journey map.

The content didn't promote the product. The content became part of the product. And millions of people began connecting with the product, initially, just to get to the content.

Much of the highest performing content in health and fitness is that which is optimized around customers' natural language. Titles like "What to Do When People Push Food on You" and "Home Workouts for Bad Knees" drive customer engagement by mirroring customers' own words back to them, letting them know that we understood what they're going through and slotting right into their preexisting mental categories for "Things I Already Care About."

Online Listening

Online listening involves literally hearing your customers' conversations, online. I spend a lot of my time on blogs, discussion boards, social media channels, media outlets, and ecommerce sites reading the comments, questions, rants, raves, and reviews of Transformational Consumers.

It is one of the least expensive, most efficient forms of customer research around. It's especially helpful for spotting what customers want, how they feel, how they want to feel, what they think they need, their research-related micro-moments, and their natural language.

For a scrappy, step-by-step primer on online listening on such sites as Amazon and Quora to get actionable insights to grow your business, do a Google search to get to the *SumoMe* blog and read "Growing a Site from 0 to 10k Visitors a Month: Sarah Peterson Edition."[5]

What Customer Research Looks Like in Real Life

At TCI, we have a very specific process for this sort of customer research, though it varies based on the company we're working with, its needs, and the brief:

1. We metabolize existing customer data and work with the company to make sure we're asking the right research question to get answers that will actually help the business.

2. We use behavioral and observational methods to recruit subjects and conduct the research.

3. We build a map and additional frameworks depicting the customer journey, segmenting the stages, and isolating any levers or phenomena we see as critical to understanding the customer.

4. We spot and document patterns in the things that help people make progress from stage to stage, get stuck, or even revert to earlier stages.

5. We validate our qualitative insights with market research, survey data, or product usage or other quantitative data.

6. We then apply a proprietary framework we call The Delta (after the Greek symbol for change) to each of these progress triggers, obstacles, quit points, rules of thumb, and decision traps. This step is critical. The gist is that we take what we know about the company, its pressing priorities and business challenges, and develop a set of strategic recommendations. Each recommendation is a specific, actionable opportunity for the company to use behavioral science, persuasive product and content design, or coaching/change management to (a) power tweak its existing offerings or (b) create new products or marketing campaigns that will create the behavior change that its customers seek.

7. We create a curriculum and multimedia assets, teaching teams their customer journey in a way that aligns with their everyday work and problem solving. In this step, we often program permanent elements into company culture, communications, and events.

Building the Skill of Customer Journey Mapping

For most companies, the skills needed to do customer research and journey mapping well and actionably are not a core competency, so hiring a research firm that will embed within your team for a time may make sense.

If you would like to learn customer research skills or want your team to have them, visit TransformationalConsumer.com to explore our training and workshops and explore the field of design thinking.

And read *Mental Models: Aligning Design Strategy with Human Behavior* by Indi Young (2008).[6] It's a masterful presentation of how to methodically approach modeling customer mindsets for product design, but content strategists, marketers, and executives can greatly benefit from Young's approach to design thinking and modes, as well.

That was a mouthful. And the truth is, a complete customer journey map is an eyeful. Download an example map of the customer journey from broke and in debt to being a good steward of their financial assets at, TransformationalConsumer.com/brokesamplejourney.

The One Rule of Customer Research

There's no one single way to do customer research that will work perfectly for every company. But there is one singular rule for customer research I want you to leave with: *do it*.

Do it because there's no way to transcend a transactional relationship with your customers, to focus on their problem the way we know is so essential, without understanding that customer and that problem.

Do it because it behavior change is illogical and hard, and if you're relying on guesses about what does and doesn't work, you will almost certainly guess wrong. People are not always rational.

Do it because, although data is one way to understand people, it is only one way. Same with demographics. Neither are enough. And relying on either, without talking to real-life human customers, is a dangerous path. The opposite is also true: the best case scenario is to develop a smart hybrid of quantitative and qualitative inputs to your new understanding of your customer.

Level Up Your Question

The fastest way to suck all the transcendence-empowering juice right out of customer research is to start that research with the wrong question and specifically with the wrong level of question. Internal research teams can find it very hard to resist this temptation, especially if the company has never done research before, if they are not skilled researchers or if the company is motivated to do research by a pressing business dilemma.

A skilled external research provider can help you level up your question, in terms of both granularity and how useful the output will be. Note that these levelings up are totally related. Usually, the first begets the second. The higher level the question, the more powerful it is.

The psychology professor turned customer-research guru Jerry Olson once told me a story about a project his team did with Cheerios some years back, illustrating the value of leveling up your research question. Originally, the Big Food empire General Mills presented to the team at Olson Zaltman asking a pretty tiny question: what was the best way to market Apple Cinnamon Cheerios?

Olson and team made the case that that wasn't the right question to be asking. They felt it was too small a question to ask and would not likely generate very impactful results. After some back-and-forth, the wise folks at General Mills agreed, and the collective team arrived at a new, higher-level question: How do people experience breakfast?

I won't go into the secret sauce of the Olson Zaltman process, except to say that it is elegant and thoughtful and goes deep. But in the course of the process, someone in a customer group pointed out that what General Mills calls "yellow box Cheerios" is generally the very first food children learn how to feed themselves.

Ah.

The Olson Zaltman team went down the research path around a partic-ular category of transformations that show up in a family, often around breakfast: a series of first-time experiences that signal an evolution in the relationship between parent and child.

The research was so powerful in its revelations that General Mills built an iconic series of television ads around it. In one, the transformation showcased was the first time you notice your child displaying empathy, and in the ad, a very young child brings his dad a bowl of Cheerios because he's worried about his father's heart health.

Cheerios positioned itself indelibly in the minds of a whole generation of Americans by surfacing how elemental it already was to these precious, universal family moments and to customers' Aspirations around healthy child development and parent-child relationships.

When you hit on the right level of question, the answers get very inter-esting, from the perspective of sparking new ideas for product, marketing, and service innovation. One resource I go to time and time again is Warren Berger's book *A More Beautiful Question: The Power of Inquiry to Spark Breakthrough Ideas* (2014).[7]

What People Say vs. What People Do

In 2015, the Corn Refiners Association published a report called *Sweeteners 360*, from which I quote: "More than 50 percent of consumers say they are actively pursuing a healthy lifestyle and avoid sugars. However, actual purchase data reveals that they still buy sweetened products at the same rate as other segments."[8]

Especially in health customer research, people often say they want one thing but actually prefer another thing in practice. A great research team will also deploy behavioral scientific methods beyond literal Q&A to get at the subconscious wants, needs, progress points, and sticking points of your customers.

The Importance of Thoughtful Outputs

It's very common to see customer-research projects culminate in customer personas or profiles, sometimes with names and photos. It's also common for our client companies to be seeking brand or product messaging, positioning, go-to-market strategy, and competitive depositioning deliverables.

These are natural outputs of customer journey research.

But the possible outputs and deliverables are vastly bigger and more impactful than even these important things. A thoughtful set of outputs and deliverables make the difference between a resource-sucking research boondoggle and a transformative experience that reinvents the company's relationship with your customers.

Of course, there should be some sort of presentation that relates the results of your customer research and shares the map of your customer journey beautifully and powerfully. Multimedia content strategy and change management are just as core a part of what we do at TCI as the research itself.

It's imperative to translate research outputs into the company's terms, into your team's natural language, into the challenges they face in operating their parts of the business.

As you conceptualize how to pull this off, here are some guideposts we generally follow.

Immersive, Interactive Content Strategy

Keep in mind that the goal is to create a lasting change in the way all the employees in your company understand the customer and in the perspective from which they begin their thinking about how to solve your customers' problems.

Create time, space, and content for your teams to be immersed in your customer journey, research, and any resulting recommendations. The content itself must be engaging, galvanizing, narrative, and interactive. It should be presented in multiple media formats: experiential, print, audio, visual, digital, online, and off. The content should trigger your employees' existing mental categories for the issues they care about. It should make clear which insights and recommendations map to the business objectives and key performance indicators, or KPIs, each team is responsible for.

Craft a Well-Designed Change-Management Process

To reorient your team around your customers and their journeys involves a long-term company-wide learning experience and transformation. It is not a one-off project. There is a deep body of knowledge about what works to create lasting company change—use it as a springboard for developing a process to deliver your research outputs in a way people can incorporate and mobilize around. Or engage someone who understands organizational change management and can help you create a process that doesn't just deliver the content but ensures its uptake.

Many Teams, One Journey

Every team in your company must be immersed in the same customer journey and research content, from research and development to product and engineering, and even marketing and operations. Now, you may very well need versions of the journey line or research deliverables that target the specific challenges and opportunities of a given team. You may also want to zoom in on a particular stage of the journey or even a particular micro-moment for an individual division or team.

But you must also create a single, holistic experience of the customer journey that all teams engage with, together. One thing we do as a matter of practice is ensure that we incorporate members from all teams as we proceed through the research and journey-mapping process. At every stage, we share preliminary results and engage every team in a conversation about what we're finding.

Doing so gets precious input and help resolving open questions from people who have likely been doing this work for a long time. It also communicates that this process is not necessarily intended to make people scrap everything they know but rather to shift perspective from product-first to Problem-First. More importantly, it organically creates a company-wide team of many change agents who have participated in the process and will become long-term advocates for bringing the research into their teams' work long after the first version of the journey map is delivered.

What you don't want is for your product and development teams to be working from a journey line that represents your customers' life cycle *with your product*, while your marketing team is working from a journey line that involves the customers' real lives in the real world. That's exactly how companies that could be transformers end up health-washing a product that has no real transformational utility for customers. And *that*, in turn, is how Transformational Consumers end up calling foul on brands that claim they are healthy or wealthy or wise making but are in fact junk food or encourage late fees or promote bad decisions.

Institutionalize Your Customers, Their Journey, and Research into Your Recurring Cultural Events and Internal Communications

All sorts of brilliant, beautiful content and experiences work for different teams to understand their customer journeys. I know a pharmaceutical company that has created a hundred personas based on the real stories of people living with the disease its products treat. Every new employee is given a patient to "be" during the first week on the job, complete with content about that patient's journey, including complications, symptoms, and medical decisions that must be made.

Pinterest does a masterful job of incorporating customers into its regular company communications. Every time a new feature is released, the product team presents that feature to the whole company from the vantage point of its impact on actual customers' experience using the product and living their life.

Rethinking your customers involves understanding their journeys, deep diving into what gets them stuck and unstuck, and crafting a process that gets off to the right start but also closes with an immersive, experiential, ongoing "finish." This internal shift has the potential power to ripple out into some massive repercussions for how you communicate with, reach, and engage customers, externally.

In keeping with the theme that what got you here won't get you there, let's explore the next natural shift along your company's journey to transcendence: rethink your marketing.

CHAPTER SEVEN

Rethink Your Marketing

Omnia vincit amor. (Love conquers all.)

—VIRGIL, APPROXIMATELY 37 BC

TRANSFORMATIONAL TAKEAWAYS

1. Transformational marketing is not stories about your brand.
2. Transformational marketing is high-value content about your customers and for their journeys.
3. Follow undying principles of human motivation and content to build brand love and engage your customers with content.

Hark back, if you will, to the very first words of this book. They were written in 1759 by the cultural critic Samuel Johnson. I imagine that shortly after he wrote that most advertising is ignored, the creative director from his ad agency rang him up. "The problem," the creative director would have said, with eyes intent through his retro-futuristically bold eyewear, "is that we need *one big idea*. We need to tell a big story about the brand! Something sensual, something *emotional*. We need to stop worrying so much about selling stuff. Stop worrying about metrics and data. Let's focus on telling some beautiful brand stories. Yes, it will cost ten million ducats to get started, but trust me—it's an annuity that will pay off well into the 1800s."

Most marketing conversations these days center around such terms as "omnichannel" and "programmatic" or such topics as the ever-evolving field of social media channels and the need for brands to produce clicky content. Many more conversations are waving a red flag that we're possibly approaching Peak Content. According to TrackMaven, brand-produced content was up 35% in 2015, while consumer engagement with that content was down 17%.[1]

Out of the fear of the unknown digital future, and in the thrall of the infinite universe of digital tools, we businesses, brands, and marketers are playing a dangerous game. We are in danger of buying the fallacy that this disengagement issue is a digital one, which will have a digital solution. This argument goes that consumers are overwhelmed by digital, fatigued by Facebook, and exhausted by email. If that is true, it would follow, then the solutions should also be digital. The Next New Social Media Platform will save the day, if you can just get it right.

Or maybe just build an app. *Yeah.* An app will fix everything. Right?

No. Nope. I am a digital and content marketer. On net, I have mostly worked on digital brands and products. I know digital and believe in digital. And I know the dirty little secret of digital: that apps have an even harder time engaging customers than nondigital products do.

Remember, Samuel Johnson was bemoaning ad overwhelm and Peak Content back in 1759. Before digital was even a thing. This problem of customers failing to engage with marketing content is not a digital issue. Digital did not cause it. And digital will not, on its own, solve it, either.

This is a human issue.

And the solutions? They will be human, too.

Human Clues to the Engagement Solution: Our Eyes, Brains, and Hearts

We humans have three body parts that give us away when something has captured our attention or we care about it a lot: our eyes, our brains, and our hearts. Each one gives us some clues to how we can rethink our marketing to engage and drive change for our customers.

In eye-tracking studies, television viewers avoided over 60% of commercial messages simply by turning their heads.[2] This doesn't even account for time-shifted viewing and the fact that most people no longer even watch broadcast television.

Upshot: people are extremely disengaged from messages about products and about brands.

Neuroscientists have found that well-told, character-driven stories excite many different centers in the brain and cause the release of oxytocin, the same hormone that releases when we bond with our dogs, babies, and sex partners.[3]

Upshot: stories engage people like nothing else. Stories in which we are the protagonist, the hero, are the most engaging stories of all.

And now, onto our hearts. Kevin Roberts, then-CEO of the global ad agency Saatchi and Saatchi, wrote the book *Lovemarks: The Future beyond*

Brands (2005).[4] He asserted that there is an echelon of companies that transcend brand status, in that their customers are loyal beyond all reason, out of all proportion to the actual usefulness of the product. To become a lovemark, a company must earn the highest levels of their customers' love *and* respect.

In Roberts's lovemark framework, without high love and high respect, a company is just a product (low love, low respect), just a fad (high love, low respect), or just a brand (low love, high respect).[5]

Even in this era of epidemic disengagement, we all know these companies, these lovemarks. They do exist: there are companies that manage to escape disengagement, companies with customers who are rabidly loyal, deeply devoted, and vocally enamored with their products, to an "irrational" degree, to an emotional degree.

Whole Foods. Starbucks. American Express. Nike.

Roberts said that the sign of a lovemark is this: when customers can't get their hands on the product of one of their lovemarks, things get out of control. They raise a hue and cry. They protest. They are outraged.

But I always thought this a curious criterion, as success metrics go. If you succeed at building a lovemark, you'll know it because . . . people will be irate if and when they can't get your product?

Fortunately, there are lots of other ways brand love shows up in a business, ways that are measurable, that provide clear direction for how we can make it happen and clear direction for course correcting our efforts when they don't seem to be working. The value of brand love for every business, no matter size or industry, and the way it shows up, is in the form of customer engagement.

Customer engagement translates into all manner of metrics that matter, depending on the type of product or the initiatives of the business you're looking at (see table 5). Beyond these metrics, there are two high-level customer-engagement metrics that matter to every business, small or large, regardless of what the product is or whether or not they are currently being tracked: word-of-mouth referrals and customer lifetime value. An engaged customer buys more of what you sell over time *and* tells their friends to buy it, too.

Table 5 How to Quantify the Love of Your Customers for Your Brand, Business, and Offerings: Brand Love / Customer Engagement Metrics, by Type of Product or Channel

Consumer packaged good or paid product

	Digital product	Digital, content, and social media channels
Repeat purchases	Daily, weekly, and monthly active users	Blog and website visits and views
Reviews and other user-generated content	Time on-site / in app	Email opens and click-through
Product usage	App-store ratings and reviews	Likes, shares, and comments

MyFitnessPal grew to over 100 million users with no paid marketing because people who used it loved it and told other people about it. If you are at a larger business, net promoter score (NPS) is probably the best way of tracking how likely your customers are to tell others about your brand or product: this is a critical engagement metric.

Smaller businesses might just ask customers how they learned of the business and try to keep track of trends in word-of-mouth referrals.

Content Engages

There's one way to engage your customers more frequently and often more emotionally than any product on its own can do: with content.

Think about it: there are only so many people who will ever track their food or their finances consistently. There are only so many times in a day, week, month, or year that people can or will go sit in a workshop or class or buy an item from a given category of consumer goods, whether it's food, paper products, or apparel.

But there is an activity that Transformational Consumers engage in on a near-constant basis, which creates literally millions of opportunities for brands to connect with them in a way that eases their transformational frictions, inspires them, and exponentially builds brand love *even* when the product is not in their presence.

Transformational Consumers Read, Watch, and Listen to Content about Their Aspirations, All Day, Every Day

And great content, it turns out, changes lives *and* drives engagement. The circle of Transformational Consumers who can and will consume well-executed content about and for their own Aspirations on any given day is vastly larger than the circle who will engage with a given product or even content about the brand.

This brings us to how, precisely, you must rethink your marketing:

From: Beautiful stories about your brand

To: High-value content about and for your customers and their Aspirations

The Gospel of Content

Shortly after it was announced that MyFitnessPal was being acquired by Under Armour, I flew to Under Armour's sprawling Baltimore campus to meet my new colleagues and brief them on our app, our community, and our programs.

En route to my first official Under Armour meeting, my tour guide walked me, in my uniform fit-and-flare dress, cashmere cardigan, and metallic sandals, through the company gym. I love a good workout and said so. She took great care to pinpoint the lower floor, to which I could see no access stairs, explaining, "If you want to get in or out, you climb the rope. Be careful to never work out so hard while you're down there that you can't get yourself back out."

Noted.

En route to my first meeting, we entered a low-slung office building, passing the cafeteria and an indoor basketball court (with a game in progress). Next we passed an exact replica of one of the company's brand stores, complete with the next season's gear on the racks and Under Armour's branded scent barely detectable as we walked by.

My guide dropped me off at a conference room, where a dozen gentlemen (all kitted out in Under Armour gear) rose to meet me. Chatting casually while we waited for everyone to arrive, their eyes darted back and forth between our conversation and an NBA game live-streaming on a laptop on the conference table.

To break the ice and start the meeting, someone suggested we go around the room and answer these questions: "What is your favorite piece of creative ever? And what do you love about it?" (To translate for those of you who don't work in marketing, advertisers often use the term "creative" as a noun, meaning a work of commercial art, such as an ad, a video, or even text: copy.)

We went around the room, and people started telling about the ads they loved in their childhood, such as the "Be like Mike" campaign. Others shared campaigns that resonate strongly with them today, including Under

Armour's own acclaimed "I will what I want" campaign, in which the prima ballerina Misty Copeland reads excerpts from numerous ballet-school rejection letters while video rolls showcasing her grace and athletic prowess.

Then it was my turn.

"Hi, guys. I'm Tara. I'm the VP of marketing for MyFitnessPal. Thanks for having me. My favorite piece of creative of all time is the Bible. It contains powerful narrative after powerful narrative, including a series of heroes' journeys that are perfectly archetypal. I am obsessed with content that drives positive behavior change, and I don't think there's another example of a piece of content, copy really, that has driven so much behavior. And yes, some of it is negative, but massive amounts of it have been positive, too. It has inspired some of the greatest acts of mankind, the greatest kindnesses, the greatest personal-growth stories, and the most impactful works of art in human history.

"And it also inspires individual people to live their own hero's journeys every day, millions and millions of times. Has for thousands of years. That's a serious shelf life, when it comes to content. From a content perspective, it's super long but also modular. In my work, we're always concerned about getting content down to tiny increments, but the fact that this massive, long-form piece of content is able to be broken down into bite-sized bits like the verse 'Jesus wept' is really a masterful use of the written word."

I looked around the room. I saw a lot of wide eyes, one or two puzzled looks, and maybe one or two thoughtful nods. Then I made one final comment: "I also love the 'Hear What You Want' ads for Beats by Dre, especially the Serena Williams one."

Sometimes, you've gotta read the room.

Almost exactly one year later, I found myself in an office on the opposite coast of the country and on the opposite end of the look-and-feel spectrum from the Under Armour HQ. From the exterior, Pinterest's red-brick facade fit more neatly into my mental schema for offices, located as it is right in my neck of the woods: start-up land, aka San Francisco's South of Market (SOMA) district.

Pinterest is a tech company and like most tech companies has a majority-male employee base. But the company is fixated on its users, most of whom are women. And everything about the company's offices reveals that obsession, from the plywood-covered walls that are an ode to its customers' love for making and DIYing to actual handicrafts of actual users that are showcased throughout the office.

It was there that I sat down to connect with my friend and colleague the Pinterest head of communications Christine Weil Schirmer. I had gone over to Pinterest to talk to Schirmer about a particular finding of our Transformational Consumer research, which revealed that there are a handful of content platforms that are particularly beloved and constantly used by Transformational Consumers. We had taken to calling them the Transformational Platforms, and the complete list went like this: Pinterest, Yelp!, Quora, reddit, Wikipedia, and of course, Google.

I shared our findings with Schirmer, Pinterest's resident expert on the scale and substance of customer engagement on the platform. Then she shared with me some insight into the Pinterest platform and how Pinners engage with content.

Pinterest, it turns out, is not the Bible. But it does have a few things in common with the Bible, from a content perspective:

▲ **Pinterest content has a crazy-long shelf life.** Pinners actively engage with a piece of content on Pinterest for an average of 110 days after it comes onto the site. Contrast this with Twitter, for which the average shelf life of a tweet is closer to 30 minutes. Schirmer suggests that brands learn the characteristics of content that performs well on any platform that they're going to invest in, before making the investment. Because of Pinterest's extended shelf life, evergreen content outperforms newsy pins, by a lot.

▲ **The platform has sweeping, global scale.** Pinterest has 50 billion pins and one billion boards, and it grows both at the rate of 75%, year over year. So when they talk about what content works, they know of what they speak.

▲ **The most engaging content holds sacred space for users' real-life problems, dreams, and the things they want to do.** The content that engages Pinners is like the most widely known biblical content in that it helps solve what Schirmer calls "meaningful daily problems for everyone on the globe"—content that answers questions that everyday people experience in their everyday lives, such as "What should I wear?" "What should I cook for dinner?" and "What should I do with my kids?" is the content Pinners care about and pin the most.[6]

How to Create Content That Engages: Start with Your Customer's Journey

That which matters most should never give way to that which matters the least.

—THE LULULEMON MANIFESTO

Engaging content is content that people care about, content that gets their attention, that captures their interest, and in best case scenarios, that they come back to, time and time again. Engaging content gets shared and goes viral. It causes people to open your emails and to click on the links in them, to read your blog again and again, to click on your Facebook links, to watch your YouTube videos, to like your Instagram posts.

I could write a million pages about how to develop engaging content strategies and how to optimize content for engagement. I won't be doing that.

But I will provide you with a few principles that every engaging, transformational content strategy I've ever worked on, and have ever even seen, adheres to. I call them the Rules of Engagement.

One note before we dive into the Rules: don't be daunted. Don't fall prey to thinking you must master the endless parade of new social media channels and content formats in order to understand content marketing. Creating content that engages doesn't start with the channels or the social media. Those are just the tools, and they come and go. That's the part that matters the least. What matters the most is your customers and their journey.

Rules of Engagement

Rule #1: **Engaging content** *is not* **beautiful messages about your brand; content that engages is high-value content that removes resistance and triggers progress along your customers' journey.** To transcend the transactional and create content that truly engages your customers, you must give up one of the most pervasive misconceptions about content and social media. The goal is not to publish stories about your brand, no matter how big, beautiful, or emotional they might be. There is a short list of things people care about, and stories about your brand are not on it.

Instead, create content about your customers and for their journey.

This doesn't mean that your content can't be beautiful, emotional, or entertaining. It doesn't mean that your content can't be stories about interesting people or places or things. And it doesn't mean that every social media post, blog post, or video must be educational content and how-to material. In fact, the opposite is true.

It just means that the majority of the content you publish should fall within a story line that either alleviates the frictions your customers are experiencing as they try to create change or inspires and excites them about the possibilities for their lives. Remember, the role you play within your customers' stories is the role of mentor, adviser, or tool.

It also means that most of your content should be about your customers (including people like them, whether or not they are using your product), their lives, and their issues. Your content should not primarily consist of pieces that tout or promote your product. While there will definitely be times you'll need to publish blog posts that simply let people know about a new product or feature, my experience is that traffic to those sorts of content posts will get anywhere from 60% to 95% less traffic than high-value content does, when published to the exact same Transformational Consumer audience.

This is hard for some leaders to swallow, the idea that most of your content should not be about your product. But the data show the truth: most people won't see your promotional content anyway. They don't care about it, so they won't click on it.

This doesn't mean that people never want to hear about your product. It just means that most of your content should be beautifully executed, high-value content that is effective at helping them on their transformational journeys, in ways that your product implicitly and, occasionally, explicitly facilitates. Think about a story everyone knows: the tale of the Three Little Pigs. No one tells the story from the perspective of the hammer. But the hammer is essential to the story and gets used nonetheless.

Content Marketing Is a Long Game

Creating content that drives real, deep customer engagement is a long game. Don't feel like every single piece of content you create has to take someone from discovering your brand to buying it to becoming a rabid brand evangelist in 500 words.

Occasionally, a single post, email, or content campaign will actually do that. But much more often, engaging content strategies use dozens or hundreds or even thousands of pieces of content over time—content that eases the frictions or triggers progress that your customers commonly encounter on their journeys.

Rule #2: Customer journey + resistance and progress triggers + natural language = your evergreen message pillars. Engaging content strategies also feature recurring messages that collectively do two things:

1. They tell the big story of your customers' transformation.

2. They imply or suggest the role that your brand and product play in that transformation.

I call these recurring messages "message pillars," because they stay the same for long periods of time, they span across all of your content program, no matter the channel, and they build the foundation for how you or your team will execute individual content programs, campaigns, and even individual blog posts.

Every one of your message pillars should map back to something meaningful about the stages of your customers' journeys or to some significant category of the things that get them stuck and unstuck. Your message pillars can be declarations, values, or beliefs and should incorporate your company's broader vision. Think of message pillars as almost like a manifesto of sorts but for your content channels. Be bold and public about them and use them as a decision rule for what content to create and what not to.

MyFitnessPal Content Program Message Pillars

In today's world, it is much easier to live an unhealthy life than a healthy one.

The MyFitnessPal vision is one of a world where the reverse is true—a world in which "healthy" is the new normal. We help people create healthy habits by making it easier than it has ever before.

MyFitnessPal's blog, email, and social media channels deliver content that facilitates the journey from an unhealthy life to a healthier one.

We focus on eliminating frequently encountered obstacles to healthy living. We share stories and insights about what works to drive success at health goals, based on our data and our members' success. And we inspire our audiences to experiment with healthful food and fitness practices until they find something that they find fun and delightful—something that works well for them.

One other note: it is ideal for you to incorporate your customers' natural language into your message pillars and into the content you produce. At the journey-mapping stage, the power of natural language is that it gives you a vivid glimpse into the mental frames that your customers have around the problem you exist to solve and the mental frames they use when they try to solve it. When you're trying to create message pillars and content, using your customers' natural language back to them is like flicking an engagement switch in their minds.

My favorite case for using natural language comes from a what-not-to-do example. And this example comes from a grocery-store trip I took with my mom when I was nine or ten years old. As we walked through the produce section, I noticed the placard hanging above the collard greens. In fact, it said, "Collard Greens." But beneath that, the copy read, "Main ingredient in traditional Black American hot salad." Whoa. What? I was eight years old then. I am 40 years old now. I have been Black that whole time. And in those 40 years, never have I met a Black American who thinks of collard greens as salad. Collard greens are not salad! Side dish, main dish, even, but salad? Nope. (And I love salad. No offense, salad.)

The disconnect was hilarious then and is hilarious now. You have the luxury of being able to talk to your people and use their language back to them. So do that. If you don't, trust me: they'll remember.

Rule #3: **Business objectives + micro-moments = which content to put where, when.** Micro-moments tell you where online your customers tend to go at the points in their journeys when they want to know, go, do, or buy something to help them achieve their goals. This empowers you to put the right content for those stages of their journeys in the right places to reach them. Micro-moments suggest the nitty-gritty of how to execute your content programs.

This is not the simplest of exercises, in part because there are nearly endless types of content that you can create. Blog posts. Data visualizations, aka infographics. Interactive infographics. Data-based PR stories, such as surveys and study findings. Cities lists. Tips lists. Lists of what not to do. Listicles, generally. User success stories. Influencer posts. Expert thought leadership posts. Unboxing videos. Web video series. eBooks. Trend reports. Podcasts. Microsites. Email newsletters. Pinnable quotes and mantras.

Trust me when I say that I'm just getting started.

There are three fundamental factors that should line up for each piece of content and content campaign: medium, format, and substance:

▲ The medium (email, social media channels, PR, online portals, even search/seo, print) must be available to you and be one that customers are prone to consuming your type of content on. You can't and shouldn't be on every medium or channel, but you can and should try to be on as many as you can do well. It is worse for your brand to publish content lackadaisically or poorly than it is not to be on a channel at all. Also think about what medium you have unique access to, such as an email list or other way of reaching your customers.

▲ The format of the content should be optimal for the content itself, such as rich pins for your blog posts, blog posts for recipe roundups, and so on.

▲ The substance itself should solve frictions that your customers are experiencing. It should further specific objectives of the business and should be executed in accordance with high production values, your brand's voice, and storytelling basics (see sidebar).

The place where all three of these overlap is small but golden: I call it the Transformational Consumer content marketing sweet spot (see figure 1).

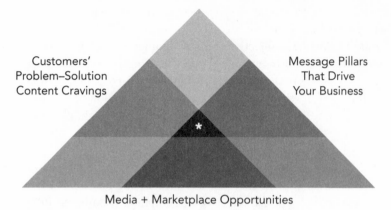

Customers'
Problem–Solution
Content Cravings

Message Pillars
That Drive
Your Business

Media + Marketplace Opportunities

Figure 1 The Transformational Consumer content marketing sweet spot

Be a Student of Story

All good marketing represents a story or is part of a larger, overarching story line. I urge my marketing teams to become lifelong students of storytelling, whether they work in media relations or creative direction or social media or email marketing.

Most of us work on mastering "story" for a lifetime. Here are some of my favorite resources to help you get there:

The Primary Instinct, a film about story, in the form of a monologue by the great character actor Stephen Tobolowsky[7]

"MasterClass on Writing," with James Patterson, MasterClass .com[8]

Nobody Wants to Read Your Sh*t: Why That Is and What You Can Do about It, by Steven Pressfield (2016).[9]

Data and Media as Decision-Aid Content: The Trulia "Rent vs. Buy Index"

A pivotal point in the journey of every would-be home buyer is one single decision: whether to rent or to buy a home. Factors such as mortgage-interest deduction, rental rates, and supply-and-demand pressures on either side make it a more complex decision than many people feel comfortable with.

At Trulia, we created a quarterly "Rent vs. Buy Index," comparing the financials of renting with those of buying in over 50 cities nationwide. Over time, the index regularly appeared in media worldwide, allowing us to drive the conversation around real estate market trends in times of recession and recovery, local market dynamics, and the personal decision factors that smart home buyers should take into account.

Rule #4: Ongoing listening + real-time content-performance data = engagement marketing. Customer research and online listening are not projects that end when the customer journey map is complete. Make them an ongoing practice. Treat all content marketing as lean marketing and build a discipline around monitoring whether and how your audiences are engaging with every piece of it. Then do more of what works and less of what doesn't. Any natural language patterns you spot will empower your teams to rapidly innovate new content topics and programs.

Rule #5: Content = R&D for product. At MyFitnessPal, our content program hit some remarkable customer-engagement milestones—and fast. We started in April, and by the following January, we had 50 million page views and 10 million unique monthly readers. We were able to increase the number of people who used the app on a given week by 22% and the number of people who used it in a given month by 24%.

We were reactivating around 500,000 lapsed users every week, just with content.

But with all that, the most exciting part of that process was that every team in the entire company was aligned around the same customer journey. So instead of us producing content about things the app couldn't actually help with, the product and engineering teams built a set of recipe-logging tools, to make it easier for people to track food when they cooked at home. They built restaurant-logging tools to help people track their food (and stay within their nutrition goals) when they ate out. And the business development team spearheaded partnerships with restaurants and menu data sources.

The Power of Obstacle-Removing Content

Content that answers the healthy-living questions that people have is the cornerstone of Thrive Market's marketing program. "We see content as marketing and marketing as content. They're ubiquitously the same thing for us," Gunnar Lovelace, co-CEO of Thrive Market, told me about the rocket-ship start-up's approach to editorial and social media programs. Lovelace and I had been talking every few months since the Transformational Consumer–focused company launched in 2014, rapidly hitting milestones of scale on its "mission to make healthy living accessible and affordable to everyone."[10]

Thrive Market is a fee-based ecommerce platform that delivers over 4,000 healthy living, food, and household products to members at a 25%–50% discount compared with retail. If Costco had a baby with Whole Foods and Amazon, Thrive Market would be the offspring.

In 2016, the company went from launch to $40 million in sales, hit two million site users, booked over 150,000 paid memberships, and gave away 150,000 free memberships to low-income families, students, teachers, and active military through its Thrive Gives program.

"What's so interesting about health and wellness products is that access is a function of price, geography, and education," Lovelace explained. To overcome the barrier of education, Lovelace explained, Thrive Market "provides content that informs, inspires, and educates people about health and wellness wherever they are in the conversation. There are consumers that are very educated about health and wellness, but there's this huge wave of new consumers entering into the health and wellness conversation for the first time. We engage these people with content on more basic levels, with written and recipe and video content."

Lovelace went on, "We cover things like how to read a label, how do carbs turn into sugar, and why you should care about green-engineered cleaning supplies. Content marketing is the right thing to do as a business, but it's also the smart thing to do. It's a huge investment on our part. We've got 15 people in our editorial team and hundreds of content creators that we manage. Our content drives a lot of engagement and value to our members. It makes us more than purely a product-based ecommerce platform."

Beyond creating value for members, Lovelace stands by the Thrive Market content program as a strategy that allows the company to connect and engage directly with its beloved customers. "A lot of people don't know that the largest magazine in the country is Costco, with eight and a half million, in terms of the circulation. With the ability to get our content directly to consumers on the Internet, we're now able to have conversations with them about issues that would have traditionally been edited, limited, or controlled by the advertiser interests on a traditional publisher network. Today we're getting 15 million page views a month—and that's growing very quickly. We expect to be a major voice long term around natural products in a way that helps shape the conversation and a way that protects and serves consumer interests long term."

The numbers back him up. Thrive Market has, itself, thrived.

Your content and marketing can connect with your customers, too. Make it about them, not your brand, and follow the Rules of Engagement.

CHAPTER EIGHT

Rethink Your Competition

If we can keep our competitors focused on us while we stay focused on the customer, ultimately we'll turn out all right.

—JEFF BEZOS

TRANSFORMATIONAL TAKEAWAYS

1. Your competition is not another company or product. Your competition is anything and everything that interferes with your customers' progress.
2. Focusing on other companies and products is also bad for your team, in other ways.
3. Transformational Consumers are particularly good at detecting when you care more about competing with another company than about their lives.

When I led marketing at MyFitnessPal, I often got the question "who is your competition?" I think people expected me to rattle off a list of other nutrition-tracking smartphone apps, and of course, there are some out there. Others probably thought any other digital fitness app was our competition, and indeed, there are a few wearable activity trackers that have nutrition-tracking functionality in their apps. Still others probably assumed that any weight-management program was our rival.

I suspect that about 100% of those who asked me this question were surprised at my answer. When I was asked this question, I would tell my inquisitor that our mission as a company was to make it easier to live a healthy life than an unhealthy one, reversing the status quo balance of global forces for and against healthy living. So, I'd say, our real competition is not any other app or tracker or company. Our real competition is anything that makes it harder to live a healthy life.

Our chief competition, then, is biology. Fat tastes good. Sugar is delicious. Our brains are wired to want more of both, the more we eat.

Also, we have to eat, all the time. Consuming food is not a behavior that you can quit cold turkey. Because we have to do it so frequently, it's natural

112

to eat habitually, to be on food autopilot. And food autopilot, eating without thinking about what you're eating, is the enemy of creating mindful, healthy eating habits.

It's just biology. But we had more competition than just biology.

Our competition was also the billion-dollar advertising and marketing budgets of fast food, processed food, and junk food.

Our competition was the fact that healthy food is actually more expensive than unhealthy food is, in many situations and locations.

Our competition was also the fact that it's so much easier to find and eat unhealthy food than it is to procure and prepare healthy food, in much of the country—and, increasingly, in much of the world.

And our competition was the truth that even if you are trying very hard to create healthy food habits, you almost can't escape unhealthy food. I defy you to try to check out at a home-improvement store without having to pass a spread of candy bars at the register. And you definitely can't go to most workplaces in America without having to run a gauntlet of birthday cakes, Monday-morning donuts, and the dreaded holiday potluck table.

So every time someone asked me who our competition was, I'd share some version of this list of phenomena that we, as a company, were running up against.

Usually, by the end, my friend would be speechless. "But yeah," I'd say, "I read somewhere that Weight Watchers sees *us* as *their* competition. Is that what you mean?"

You Can't Serve Two Masters

I recognize that my point of view on competition is a contrarian one. Not to get all biblical about it, but you can't serve two masters. When you orient your entire team around an intense focus on the competition, your company operates in a constant state of distractedness from your customers, their lives, their personal disruption initiatives, and all the opportunities you have to facilitate them.

To kick-start a two-way love affair with Transformational Consumers, you must undertake a major, directional shift in the way your entire company conceives of "competition."

From: Your competition as another company, product, app, or service.

To: Your competition is every point of friction that your Transformational Consumer audience is likely to encounter on their journeys.

Sure, *someone* in your company needs to understand the marketplace: who your competition is, what other products are on the market, and how they are doing, at a basic level. But there's a point at which paying attention to other companies and what they're doing interferes with your team's ability to immerse itself in the world of your consumer, to innovate solutions to the frictions and quit points they encounter, and to focus on creating authentic story lines about why and how you exist to help them experience life more healthfully, more prosperously, and more wisely.

The traditional approach that companies take to "the competition" seems to have carried over from the high school football field. I've seen companies operate in utter fixation on their competitors' every move, watching and dissecting their product launches with the same focus they might once have watched film of the other teams' games, in an effort to get a sense for what's in their playbook.

I've also witnessed executive teams take this even further, attempting to get their entire workforce to rally around the prospect of having a big, shared enemy, in the form of one or more competitors.

Apple's chief design officer, Jony Ive, has been quoted as cautioning that "people can sense care and can sense carelessness." When you care too much about your competitors, it necessarily translates into some degree of carelessness about your customers. And they can sense that: your customers can, and so can your employees. And the ones who can sense that carelessness the most are the Transformational Consumers in both your internal and external audiences.

Transformational Consumers Compare Products across a Competitive Set in More Rapid Cycles than Other Customer Groups Do

Part of what makes people qualify as Transformational Consumers is that they frequently buy things from different companies that might help them succeed along their behavior-changing, life-improvement journeys—some of which are lifelong.

People who are in the market for workout gear, for example, are likely to make repeated purchases of athletic apparel across multiple brands, for years and years. They are likely to wear multiple brands in the same outfit and from workout to workout within the same week. As a result, they can compare how a particular item or brand looks, feels, and functions across workouts against other products by their own observations in a short period of time and sometimes on the same day, simply by trading notes with their workout buddies. There is often emotional charge and meaning assigned to the brands and products that make something difficult more beautiful and more fun, and the copycat apparel brands that don't perform well trigger similarly intense emotions on the other end of the spectrum: ridicule and disdain, among them.

This is not how people consume nontransformational items such as, say, conventional laundry soaps. But because of Transformational Consumers' rapid and frequent comparison cycles, it is easier for them to spot when a company tends to create "me too" products or products that prioritize form over function in an effort to compete with other companies than it is for other customer groups or for their purchases in nontransformational, more commoditized products and services.

Transformational Consumers Are Highly Skeptical of Big Companies' Claims That Their Products and Services Are Beneficial

Transformational Consumers have a long memory. They remember when margarine was supposed to be great for us to eat . . . and when it turned out that margarine was the devil's work. They are extremely skeptical of Big Food companies and what they see as the sordid historical legacies of food processing, genetic crop modification, and "health-washing" labels to sell food items on the basis of health claims.

Every time a Big Food company with a history of selling unhealthy foods claims to be turning over a healthier leaf in an effort to stave off competition from healthier brands and declining market share from healthier social norms, Transformational Consumers' lie detectors come out.

Deep, Noble Missions and Authentic Story Lines Appeal to Transformational Consumers

Products and marketing inspired by beating the competition are rarely noble. When your company launches product or marketing campaigns primarily to compete with someone else, the story line behind the offering will tend to be surface deep and might even read to Transformational Consumers as inconsistent with the rest of your business or untrue to your company's history.

When your competitive focus, as a company, is trained on eliminating your customers' obstacles to healthier, more prosperous lives, you might do things that seem weak, competitively, but Transformational Consumers will see as strong, authentic, lovable statements of what you stand for: them.

In 2014, the pharmacy giant CVS placed one very costly such stake in the ground, when it became the first national retail pharmacy chain to take cigarettes and other tobacco products off the shelves of its 7,700 locations across the United States, on the following grounds: "the sale of tobacco products is inconsistent with our purpose—helping people on their path to better health."[1]

The projected revenue hit? Two billion dollars in lost annual revenues from tobacco products, not to mention the incidental purchases smokers would no longer make at CVS while buying cigarettes.[2]

The policy was implemented as part of the company's overall rebrand from CVS/caremark to CVS/health and its express intention to grow its identity as a health-care provider to consumers and to other critical health-related audiences, from physicians to insurance companies. In the policy's first year, it is estimated to have resulted in people smoking 95 million fewer packs of cigarettes in 13 states.[3]

While the revenue hit was significant, the company's other lines of business soared, offsetting the tobacco losses handily. Overall revenues were up 10% in the policy's first year, right on target.[4]

How to Shift Your Company's Concept of "The Competition"

It's relatively easy to stop propagandizing the war with another product or company internally, especially from leadership levels on down. Just stop setting goals by reference to other companies. Minimize how much meeting time is devoted to talking about competitive companies and products. Discourage product-design approaches that focus first on assessing or iterating what is already out there.

That's the easy part.

Reinvesting the human resources and mindshare of your teams to focus on a new class of competition—eliminating the frictions and obstacles of your Transformational Consumer—is much more challenging.

Fortunately, it turns out to be an adventure that immediately flicks the mental switches of interest and engagement in your employees and pays off in fresh innovations that your customers are much more likely to try, use, adopt, and evangelize over the long term.

There are three redirects you'll need to undertake to make this shift throughout your teams: focus on "your people," their problems, and solving their problems from first principles.

1. Focus on Your People

If you've already worked through chapter 6, you should have a relatively clear understanding of who your audience is, as (re)defined through the Transformational Consumer lens.

For purposes of shifting your competitive focus, your people include the following:

a. Everyone out there who is trying to solve the health, financial, career, lifestyle-design, or personal-growth problem that your company aims to solve (whether or not they are your customers, currently)

b. Everyone out there who is trying to upgrade their lives for the healthier, wealthier, and wiser, in a way that your products or services can facilitate (whether or not they are your customers, currently)

c. The people who are likely to send groups (a) and (b) your way.

At this stage of the game, you've articulated your target audiences through the lens of their lifestyle-design and personal disruption objectives, the ones you hope to help them with. Now let's build on that by focusing on these people as we reconstruct the way you think about your competition.

I mean that very literally. The goal at this step is simple—your challenge is to fill in the blank of the statement "Our competition is _____" in a way you've never done it before.

If you're like most companies, you would normally fill in that blank with another company's name, the name of a competitive product, or even a stock symbol.

In rethinking your competition through the lens of the Transformational Consumer, you'll need to fill in the blank with a phrase that equates to "everything that stops your people from succeeding at the particular personal disruption initiative(s) your business or product exists to help solve." You can be general on the "everything" until Step 2. But get as specific as you can when it comes to "your people" and their personal disruption objectives.

If you are a financial firm, for example, your statement might be "Our competition is anything that stops people from saving the money they need to retire."

If you run a chain of low-cost, neighborhood fitness studios, you might say your competition is "the everyday forces that stop people from getting regular exercise."

If your company publishes online educational courses for people who want to start small creative businesses, such as graphic design and photography, you could envision your competition as "anything that makes it harder for beginning designers and photographers to succeed as creative entrepreneurs."

Here's a real-life example we can workshop through all three steps of rethinking the competition: REI has built its entire business to inspire, educate, and outfit its members for a "lifetime of outdoor adventure and stewardship."[5] So the company might phrase its "competition" statement as "anything that stops people from being able to enjoy the great outdoors." Now, do yours.

Our competition is _____.

2. Focus on Your People's Problems

In our exploration of defining your people, your target audience, and your customers through the Transformational Consumer lens, developing an ongoing market intelligence or customer-insights research program is essential (see chapter 6 for much more detail on why you must do this and how). One of the most valuable takeaways from your insights practice is the deep understanding of the decision traps, pitfalls, friction spots, and quit points that your people frequently encounter on their journeys.

The process of rethinking your competition creates another use of the insights from your customer research. Now you can level up the specificity of the way you talk about your competition, by putting it in the terms of the specific challenges that your people face that your company, your product, your technology, or even your content and communications programs can help with.

In other words, their obstacles are your competition. Make sure you're not looking solely for their obstacles to buying or using your product—you're trying to get at all the frequently occurring dramas and obstacles on the path from unhealthy eating to healthful eating or the roadblocks people experience on the path from struggling to save to ready to retire.

Gather your understanding of your people's specific roadblocks from every source available: from user data, surveys, ethnographic research, and even third-party data. Online listening and subject-matter experts can also be of great help.

Once you have an understanding of the specific issues that frequently arise as roadblocks to your customers' success at their HWW goals, you can use it to talk about your competition more specifically and in a way that begins to inspire internal conversations, innovation, and external communications.

REI, for example, knows that intimidation is one big reason people don't venture into outdoor sports, and another is that they don't always have someone to venture out with. The retail collective also recently realized that one of the reasons people go outdoors less in the wintertime, even in California and other warm-weather climates, is that they are stressed about buying gifts and scoring the best deals around the holidays.[6]

These are obstacles the company has created market-leading solutions for, which it might not have if it was focused on competing against another gear retailer. But we'll come back to that.

First, let's turn back to CVS. Let's say a customer who smokes wants to get healthier by quitting. If she comes to the pharmacy to buy a nicotine patch, but the pharmacy also has cigarettes for sale, the in-your-face availability of those cigarettes is a pretty serious obstacle to her effort to quit, isn't it? We'll come back to this one, too.

There's a reverse approach you should also factor in: take the things that you know work to help your people succeed, and consider the enemies of those success factors your competition, too.

At MyFitnessPal, for example, instead of paying too much attention to Weight Watchers, we viewed our competition as everything that makes it harder to live a healthy life than an unhealthy one. One thing we knew was that habitual, mindless eating—eating and drinking without thinking—is one of the biggest obstacles to healthy living. And we also knew from our customers, ethnographies, and published scientific data that food tracking successfully unclicks people off food autopilot, forcing them to think about what they eat and when they eat it and driving almost immediate change to eating habits.

But we also knew that food tracking is just a difficult habit, in itself, to build, precisely because eating is so frequent, so habitual, and so thoughtlessly done, the vast majority of times.

So for our product-development team, everything that would make it difficult for someone to use food tracking to get off food autopilot, eat with more mindfulness, and develop the nutritional literacy and healthier eating habits that food tracking facilitates became that team's competition.

See, the most powerful Transformer companies engage in this customer-obstacle-focused slant of "competitive analysis" on a never-ending cycle:

▲ Understanding the obstacles their customers face

▲ Learning how and where people get stuck

▲ Solving those problems

▲ Understanding how people overcome the obstacles and get unstuck

▲ Understanding what stops others from achieving this success

▲ Solving those problems

▲ And so on and so forth

At Transformer companies, this is just called executing against mission, product design, marketing—the core functions of a team, all oriented to obliterate the enemy: their customers' obstacles.

3. Focus on First Principles

This is where the power of this rethink really manifests itself in your business: when you can harness the focal and energetic shift away from what other companies are doing, redirect it to your customers, and use that to innovate products and messaging from first principles.

When you focus on competitors, you run the risk of their activities and approaches infiltrating yours, which often leads to me-too products that purport to compete or iterate something that may or may not have been effective for your people in the first place.

When I use the phrase "first principles," I'm referring to an independent style of thinking about how to solve your customers' transformational obstacles and smooth their frictions without reference to what's already out there.

Tesla's CEO, Elon Musk, paraphrased first principles thinking well, in an interview with the serial Internet entrepreneur Kevin Rose: "I think it's important to reason from first principles rather than by analogy. The normal way we conduct our lives is we reason by analogy. [With analogy] we are doing this because it's like something else that was done, or it is like what other people are doing. [With first principles] you boil things down to the most fundamental truths . . . and then reason up from there."[7]

With first principles, you only care about solving your customers' transformational obstacles—period. You start from the problem and use your team's talents, reasoning, and skill to create new solutions to that problem, versus fixating on how it's been attacked before or what has or hasn't worked for other companies or in your own company's past.

Let's see how first principles thinking manifested itself in the companies we've seen thrive by positing their competition as their customers' transformational obstacles.

REI:

Competition is: Anything that stops people from venturing into the great outdoors.

More specifically: Intimidation, isolation, and in winter, holiday shopping pressures stop people from getting outdoors.

Innovation driven by obstacle-as-competition insight: Instead of focusing on trying to beat the sporting-goods store discounts, REI pioneered a series of classes and group excursions at all levels, from local cycling trips for beginners to hiking tours of the Greek Isles.

In 2015, REI secured massive, positive press, industry awards, and praise from Transformational Consumers with a national Black Friday shutdown of its stores. The story line went that shoppers needn't worry about missing Black Friday deals at REI because the stores would be closed so everyone could go hiking. The company carried out the campaign by shipping freeze-dried, meals ready to eat (MRE) versions of Thanksgiving dinner to thousands of its best customers and ultimately inspired donors and state and regional park organizations to offer free admissions to parks all over the country on Black Friday weekend.[8]

CVS:

Competition is: Anything that stops people along their path to better health.

More specifically: Seeing cigarettes at the pharmacy where you go to buy smoking-cessation products.

Innovation driven by obstacle-as-competition insight: Taking cigarettes and tobacco off the shelves. The $2 billion-plus revenue hit was offset by increases in other lines of business. The bigger win for public health was the 95 million fewer cigarette packs sold in key states during the first year of the ban. But for the company, perhaps the biggest win is yet to be quantified—the impact of the authentic, money-where-its-mouth-is brand message that the company now known as CVS/health has sent to the market, to consumers, and to its critical health-care referral partners, such as physicians and insurers.

Last but not least, let's come full circle to MyFitnessPal. If we had viewed Weight Watchers as our competition, we'd have probably spent a lot of time trying to do what they do, just a little better than they do it. Maybe we would have raised money to get bigger-celebrity spokespeople or tried to come up with some sort of next-generation points system.

Here's the "competition" rubric we operated under, instead:

Competition is: Everything that makes it harder for people to live a healthy life rather than an unhealthy one.

More specifically: Biology, food autopilot, the cost of healthy food, the tastiness and convenience of unhealthy food, and everything that makes it hard to build healthy habits such as food tracking and home cooking.

Innovation driven by obstacle-as-competition insight:

▲ Barcode scanner to make it easy to track packaged foods

▲ Massive food database so users never have to enter nutritional data

▲ Social features and challenges for support, accountability, and competition

▲ Recipe-logging features for home-cooked meals

▲ Content, marketing, and PR campaigns featuring user success stories, habit making and breaking advice, cost-effective recipes and cooking tutorials, and other messages tailored to remove the frictions commonly encountered on the journey from unhealthy to healthy.

And it worked. People who have even a single friend on MyFitnessPal lose twice as much weight as people who don't use the app's social features. MyFitnessPal users who log home-cooked recipes lose 40% more weight than those who don't. The barcode scanner and food database are consistently mentioned by people who have successfully used the app to lose weight, despite having been unsuccessful with all manner of diets before.

And that's a lot of people—the app's users have lost hundreds and hundreds of millions of pounds (and kilos and stone).

TRANSFORMER CASE STUDY: Hampton Creek

Founded in 2011, Hampton Creek is the world's fastest growing food company. Its products are on—and fly off—the shelves nearly everywhere that matters, from Google's Mountain View campus to Whole Foods, Safeway, Target, Kroger, Walmart, and the food-service giant Compass Group.

Because Hampton Creek is best known for its egg-free products such as Just Mayo and Just Cookie Dough, it came to me as a surprise that no one at the company ever uses the word "vegan" to describe its products. Instead, Hampton Creek's team of data scientists and Michelin-starred chefs is fixated on ensuring that its products are more delicious and less expensive than any other product on the market, not just healthy or plant-based competitors.

At a private tasting tour last year at the company's San Francisco headquarters, I talked with the head of bioinformatics, Lee Chae, a jovial gent with advanced degrees in both plant biology and data science.[9] He said the company's origins began with founder Josh Tetrick's dismay at the world's broken food system. There are upward of 200,000 edible plant species in the world, but over 90% of the world's food comes from just 12 of them. This has created a food chain that relies heavily on industrial farming of both plants and animals, creating tragic levels of industrial waste and unconscionable livestock practices.

The company's research and development team has honed in on 20 plants, such as pea protein and sorghum, that provide the gastromolecular characteristics that the company's culinary innovation team has pinpointed as elemental to delicious food mixes and condiments. The goal? To create foods that actually taste better than their conventional counterparts do and to sell for cheaper, too.

Hampton Creek sees this broken food-supply chain as its primary competitor and sees the reputation of "alternative" food products as not tasting too good as number two. No one I spoke with at the company even brought up other food companies, the more conventional "competition," in conversation. I asked a number of senior Hampton Creek staffers how they felt about the vehement response they'd incited in the food industry, including an unsuccessful campaign asking the FDA to force the term "mayo" off Hampton Creek's popular Just Mayo label.

Everyone, from Tetrick on down, was very bold about their vision vis-à-vis the food-industry "competition": a vision that other food companies would follow suit, replacing animal products in their lines after Hampton Creek demonstrated the viability and profitability of doing so.

As if on cue, in 2016, Unilever released a new eggless "mayo" product under the storied Hellman's brand. In an interview with the *New York Times*, Tetrick stayed on message, citing the development as an "extraordinarily positive thing," elaborating as he did when I spoke with him that he "didn't start Hampton Creek to do anything but try and make the food system much closer to our values and there is no way just one company can do it."[10]

What Will Happen to Your Company When You Make This Shift?

When you make this shift, new markets and opportunities will come to light. Your team will see new ways it can magically, powerfully solve problems, sometimes very, very simply.

Your team will be able to focus like never before on the single issue of your people's problem, and breakthrough innovation will result.

Your team will effortlessly spot power tweaks—small changes that can be made to existing products that make them much more desirable to or effective for your people, your audience, your customers.

You'll get clearer, company-wide, on what you are and are not about, clearer on what you do and do not do. This will naturally create organic guardrails around your team's mental bandwidth and what it should and should not be spent on.

When you get clear on what you do and do not want to focus on, as a company, you'll begin to see companies that you once saw as competitors as the "co-opetition" and spot new opportunities for partnership, synergy, and business development.

What happens to your company when you redirect your competitive energies from other products to your people, their problems, and first principles is *focus*: a long-game focus on your customers that begets engagement, internally, and innovation, externally.

I've worked with two companies that had what I saw as pathological-level focus on a competitor. The first was ultimately bought by that same exact competitor, after which the most valuable members of the acquired company immediately left, disheartened to now be a part of the very enemy on which their sights had been trained for years.

The second still boasts and builds its culture around its intense effort to beat the number-one company in its space, even as both companies and the industry itself grow significantly, year over year. This company struggles with key markets, populations, and initiatives in which its competitor consistently and impressively innovates. It also consistently puts out products that customers see as inferior copycats of others on the market, and its rate of employee disengagement is sky high. Don't get me wrong; the company performs well, revenue-wise. But who knows what it could do if its massive innovation and product-design resources were freed from focusing on keeping up with number one and allowed, instead, to focus on solving its customers' HWW journey problems and obstacles to transformation? I submit that it would be truly, deeply transformational. Counterintuitively, it might be the very thing that would allow it to best its nemesis, for once and for all.

CHAPTER NINE

Rethink Your Culture

Oh, you hate your job? Why didn't you say so? There's a support group for that. It's called *everybody*, and they meet at the bar.

—DREW CAREY

TRANSFORMATIONAL TAKEAWAYS

1. The best employees to build products and content that engage Transformational Consumers are, themselves, Transformational Consumers.
2. To retain and engage brilliant employees, leaders must create a fear-free workplace and a culture of conversation.
3. Transcending the transactional by repositioning your company as transformational doesn't just engage customers; it also reactivates and engages employees.

In most circles, it is vastly more remarkable to love your job than to hate it. I have discovered this through a career of joy tripping through a series of mostly delightful career moves, very much by design. On the couple of occasions I've taken jobs working for other people, I always approached it as though I were interviewing them for the privilege of giving them that season of my career.

That approach has paid off.

I have chosen to work only with CEOs I had a deep respect and admiration for. This respect was partly for their visions, which were aligned tightly to the things I personally care about the most. And this respect was partly for their grounded vulnerability and strong humility, for their ability to clearly communicate that they valued and needed other strong, visionary leaders to build an organization that could bring their visions to life.

I have also chosen to work for myself quite often in my career. And, somewhat counterintuitively, I have found it to be the least risky, most energizing endeavor of all.

Like many of the entrepreneurs and leaders I've worked with and known, I am definitely a Transformational Consumer. Also like many leaders I know, my career and business endeavors fall almost equally within my mental frames for healthy, wealthy, and wise. The way I show up to make an impact on the world, the way I fulfill my potential, the way I create value and wealth, and the way I live a physically and emotionally healthy life is largely by service to my employees, my clients, and their customers by virtue of how I lead and operate my business.

The same is true for employees. Most of the product developers, marketers, designers, and service providers who can deliver at the highest levels to Transformational Consumers *are themselves* Transformational Consumers. And they will exhibit that quintessential tendency of Transformational Consumers to try to fulfill their potential at all costs, to constantly level up their work lives (in terms of finance and fulfillment), and to try to fix what is broken, if their work lives are not working for them.

You can't build a company that is a powerful force for transformation and create an elevated relationship with your customers with a team of disgruntled, disengaged, stagnant employees.

And you can't build anything big or great on your own. If you feel like your work is the primary lever you can pull to make an impact on the world, then there's a lot to be said for making that impact big and making it great. If you've read this far, chances are good you've already come to this conclusion.

If you want to transcend the transactional, you must first rethink your company culture, your very team.

From: Disgruntled, disengaged employees

To: A fear-free team of brilliant beings aligned around a transformational vision and mission

I ran a very high-quality real estate brokerage practice, working one-on-one with customers. But I closed that practice down to go work with Trulia because that role would allow me to serve millions of home buyers, empowering them to make better, more easeful decisions. That scale made it an exciting endeavor.

I could be a personal trainer or life coach, and I've done those things. It's exhilarating. These are noble roles, and we need people to do them, brilliantly. But there are only so many people you can ever serve, one-on-one. At MyFitnessPal, I was able to impact the health journeys of tens of millions of people. Trust me, it is delightfully easy to go to work in the morning when you know that's what you get to work on.

The same goes for my role now. The mission of this book and of my company, in general, is to inspire and illuminate a generation of leaders and companies to understand, reach, and engage Transformational Consumers. I will declare this book successful when over 1,000 companies that serve over ten million customers each are actively using it in their programs. That's how I'll know this content is impacting billions of actual customers' lives for the healthier, wealthier, and wiser, which is the big vision for my life's work.

The long and short of it is that scale matters.

I learned early on that as an entrepreneur and executive trying to operate at scale, the true linchpin of how much impact I can have on the world is this: the brilliance, engagement, and activated creative power of my people.

Without them, I can do absolutely nothing.

If you're an impact junkie as I am, scale matters. And then team matters even more.

So, long ago I decided to become a student of what it takes to create a highly engaged, highly productive team and workplace. I learned all about strategy, all about execution. I studied what conditions people's brains and bodies need to bring and keep all of their brain cells fully online and to maintain a state of creative flow.

I learned all about the substance of my work but also that the execution-level stuff of marketing changes very rapidly. I realized that, as much of a lone ranger as I once was, you can't build anything great alone. I remembered reading, in *Good to Great*, that some companies are built on a one genius plus 100 helpers formula. At MyFitnessPal, for the first time, I built a team based on one genius plus 100 geniuses formula. And that's the formula I continue to use as we grow and build TCI.

I elected to focus on becoming a great leader, attracting the right people with a powerful vision and retaining them and keeping them engaged with clear, successful systems and a conscious workplace. I elected to focus on creating teams that fixated on our customers and their Aspirations, so we could build programs on undying Rules of Engagement while also meeting our customers right where they are—online, offline, and emotionally—at any given moment of time.

But as we began to work with larger and larger companies to reorient them around serving Transformational Consumers at ever-larger scale, I ran into a massive challenge, over and over again: that most big companies suck. This is why so many Transformational Consumer employees leave. They leave to go be personal trainers and massage therapists, to start their own Crossfit boxes and yoga studios, to be consultants (especially social media consultants). They leave to be musicians and drive for Uber or Lyft to pay the bills. They read *The 4-Hour Workweek* or *The $100 Startup* and realize they can rent out their spare rooms and houses, create whatever business they want, and live a life free of the melodramas of the modern corporate work world.[1]

This, to me, is one of the biggest tragedies of our time, that the companies with the scale, reach, and resources to most powerfully help people change their lives cannot retain or keep engaged the specific employees they need to create and deliver truly transformative products, services, and content into the marketplace—a marketplace full of Transformational Consumers who are actively seeking to connect with brands in this way.

Experience has taught me that there are a few things leaders and companies must do to attract, retain, and engage the Transformational Consumer *employees* who are the most likely to innovate for, reach, and engage Transformational Consumer *customers*:

Create a Fear-Free Workplace and a Culture of Conversation

I grew up attending all-Black, Baptist churches. But ten years ago, I found myself visiting a nearly all-white Presbyterian church in downtown Berkeley. It was a large congregation, hundreds in attendance, with a woman minister I greatly enjoyed. But it was so quiet in there, compared with my rollicking regular church experience. When prayer ended and I said "Amen" out loud, heads turned. Many heads turned.

After church, a number of people spotted me as a visitor and stopped by to shake my hand, say hello, and deliver various other warm welcomes. I mentioned my Amen faux pas to one woman, and she said, "I know—it's *so* quiet in here that my kids call us 'the frozen chosen.'"

This incident came to mind a few weeks ago, when I was at a marketing-industry leadership roundtable. There were maybe 15 of us in the room, all CMO types, mostly from Fortune 50 companies. People shared how hard it is to get employees to engage with company leaders and with each other: to share their thoughts, questions, ideas, concerns, successes, and failures with the rest of the company. One exec mentioned how afraid employees are to speak up, for fear of being criticized, singled out, or shamed. Several others said they have the same issue. Then people started trading notes on the various internal social media tools, such as Yammer and Slack, that hold the space for internal conversations.

What I thought but didn't say that day is that the problem these teams have is not a technological problem. It's a cultural problem. If people are afraid, it's because they have reason to be. If people don't share their ideas or lessons learned for fear of being singled out as having failed, chances are good that, well, they've seen someone be singled out for having failed.

This cultural problem is pervasive. I mentioned it to a close friend who has worked for a series of very large companies. She said, "Oh yeah, you don't speak up or challenge leadership. I did that on my first job and was pulled aside and told that was a CLM." "A what?" I asked. "A career-limiting move."

Also pervasive is that most people come to the workplace wounded and fearful. And most leaders are operating in fear and woundedness. If you want to serve Transformational Consumers by retaining Transformational Consumers, it then becomes your job to create a workplace that is conscious and healing, constantly inviting people to operate without the fear of losing power, losing their jobs, uncertainty, insufficient resources, and instability. It also becomes your job to work on your own emotional wounds and fears so that you can boldly take your team into a new era of transformation.

Employees who are so repressed that they think asking a question of their manager is a CLM are the "frozen chosen" of their companies: chosen because they brought some valuable knowledge or expertise to the company in the first place; now frozen because, like the parishioners at church that day, they are part of an organization in which simply saying a thing, asking a question, pushing back on a planned initiative, turns heads. It raises alarm. It has an acronym: CLM.

This is *cultural*. Black churches have their own set of issues, to be sure. But one thing many of them do well is foster a culture of conversation. Here's an anthropological experiment for you: if you've never attended a Black church, take two hours this Sunday and do so. You'll learn, quick-like, that a Black church service is not a spectator sport. Black pastors are notorious for engaging their audiences in a two-way conversation. They look for, expect, and sometimes flat-out demand audience participation from the first note of the first song to the closing benediction.

It's not for nothing that the saying "Can I get an Amen?" has penetrated the larger lexicon.

But it's not just an "Amen" that most Black church pastors want these days. Things I have actually heard Black pastors ask their audiences to do include repeat after them, punch your neighbor, tell your neighbor how great he or she looks today, touch your forehead, do a two-step, do the electric slide, rap along to an old Slick Rick song, and fill in the blanks of a not-so-old song by a guy the pastor described as the "dysfunctional poet savant Lil' Wayne." Not to be outdone, my current pastor (who is white but pastors a very diverse congregation) recently did a cooking demo onstage and had a few of the thousand people in the sanctuary come up to get their piece of the hero sandwich he'd constructed.

Good pastors—and great leaders—foster conversation because conversation fosters engagement. And engagement fosters excellence, joy, creative problem solving, and innovation in our work. It also dramatically accelerates any and every change-management experience: if you truly want to reorient your company to serve Transformational Consumers, you need buy-in at the top, but you also need change agents at every level and on every team.

This is why we generally include members from every team at various points throughout our research process, so that they are already engaged as agents for reorienting their teams around the final customer journey model and the strategic decisions that come out of it.

Here's the rub: I'll bet that, if you asked the execs in the room at that roundtable, they would say they do everything they can to encourage conversation. You can't get people to engage in an ongoing, company-wide culture of conversation just by telling them to do so, if the rest of your organization's culture has a chilling effect. Companies that understand how mission critical conversation is to the health of their teams must normalize it and enculturate conversation, deeply, with their actions.

Normalize Real Talk

You could have put Martin Luther King, Jr., himself in that Presbyterian church on that one day, and it would have turned the pin-drop hush into a momentary mutter, at most, because feedback was simply not a cultural norm in that church. Normalizing real, frank, two-way conversations takes intentional effort, modeling, and the creation of spaces that prove, over time, to be safe harbors for free expression—and I mean safe occupationally and emotionally.

You go first. And second. And fifth, if need be. Leaders should be the first to call themselves and their challenges out, conduct public postmortems, and review the lessons they've learned—and not fake ones: they should take real failures or projects that didn't quite go as planned and say so, then work through what they might do differently in the future. When you put an idea out there, ask for pushback—literally invite people to show you where you're missing something or thinking about it wrong.

Innovation-Sparking Talking Points

Download a free swipe file of my own leader scripts to kick-start your employees' most innovative thinking at TransformationalConsumer .com.

Ask people for their thinking, for their troubleshooting. Make—then honor—the rule that the best idea wins, no matter *whose* idea it is. Let employees see when the project manager's idea gets roadmapped instead of the CEO's. When employees formerly known as frozen begin to thaw and share their thinking or ideas, expressly reward the sharing and the thinking, even when you have to course correct their concept to get it closer to something actionable.

Consistently Demonstrate a High Value on Free Thinking, Questioning Authority, Pushback, and Postmortems

Once people share their thinking, consistently show them that you honor it and them for taking the risk to be vulnerable and express themselves. Allow employees' free thinking and concepts to infiltrate your company's language, culture, product roadmap, and editorial calendar. Learn to ask more beautiful questions, in response to employees' thoughts and ideas. Then ask them. Then do it all over again. Regularly.

"Can I get an Amen?" is anything but a rhetorical question at many a Black church. It's a cultural reality. If your business depends on the engagement, creativity, and free thinking of your teams, creating a culture of conversation must move from abstract ideal to a cultural reality in your organization, as well.

Operate with Constant Reference to a Clear, Transformational Vision and Mission

Make sure that your story spine, your customer journey, and the problem you exist to solve for the Transformational Consumer is reflected and reiterated in your company's vision statement. Your vision should represent the "after" state of the world, if you solve the problem you exist to solve. It should be big, measurable, and humanity level, versus flowery and hard to understand.

Jim Stengel might say that it should express the higher-order benefit that your brand gives to the world.

Next up: mission. If you want your company to serve Transformational Consumers, your mission statement should answer this question: What might we do, over and over, in order to go from the status quo problem state to the envisioned state?

Accordingly, in the world of transformational business, multiple companies might have the exact same vision and arrive at very different answers to the mission. Your mission should be based on what customers actually need and what, within your company's core competencies, you are able to do over and over that helps them progress on that journey or eliminates obstacles, frictions, sticking points, and decision traps that they commonly experience along the way.

For example, MyFitnessPal, Target, and CVS all share a vision of billions of people living healthier lives.

▲ MyFitnessPal does this by focusing on helping people build healthy food and fitness habits and helping them break unhealthy ones, over and over again, across millions and millions of people.

▲ Target does this by helping people discover and access wellness products and healthy foods wherever they're at, including at the checkout register, at an accessible price.

▲ CVS is working on this same vision by *not* forcing smokers to have to pass cigarettes to get to their smoking-cessation products.

Then, refer to and actively use your vision and mission, internally, all the time. All the time. All the time. All the time. Use it as a constant decision rubric, from strategy all the way down to tactics: Does this thing we're about to do fall within this mission? Does it further the vision?

Empower your teams to say no to projects and products at every level that pull against vision and mission, even if they will make you money. At MyFitnessPal, we frequently decided not to take money from junk-food advertisers, because it went against mission.

And yes, you do have to be a fearless leader-hero and company to do that.

Demonstrate, Require, and Reward Integrity at All Costs

One of the things Transformational Consumers hate the most about their workplaces is being ignored or penalized for pointing out what is true, what is real, when leadership simply doesn't want to hear it. This is a frequently cited cause of the work stress that causes employees to disengage or to quit, and I mention it here because it comes up a lot in times of change or reorientation in a company.

Leaders get frustrated when teams constantly bring up why a new initiative might not work, when the truth is that the teams are the closest to the customer. Rather than disregarding these employee-waved flags, we must learn to exercise what I call *constructive* integrity.

▲ Listen to the feedback, even if it gets frustrating. There might be some truth to it, and it might empower you to tweak strategy to avoid pitfalls, in advance.

▲ Then, acknowledge and value employees who call out issues in advance, while also teaching them skills around problem solving, prioritization, and creating possibilities beyond what they might ever have done or worked on before.

Get on the growth path to a culture of deep integrity, where leaders both demonstrate and reward these six elements of the author, coach, and psychologist Henry Cloud's powerful definition of integrity:

▲ Creates and maintains trust

▲ Is able to see and face reality

▲ Works in a way that brings results

▲ Embraces negative realities and solves them

▲ Causes growth and increase

▲ Achieves transcendence and meaning in life[2]

It's a path and a process. But it's also necessary, if you want to retain and keep engaged the Transformational Consumer employees you need to reach and engage Transformational Consumer customers.

Transformation → Employee Reactivation

Fortunately, one of the latent virtues of successfully reorienting a company around service to the Transformational Consumer is that, if you pull it off, it holds the potential to reactivate your employees and company culture. This is true for the same reasons everyone loves to watch a child take his or her first steps or learn how to ride a bike: watching and participating in human potential being unlocked is inherently exciting, engaging, inspiring.

It reminds you of your own untapped potential. It inspires you to get after it, whatever your own "it" may be. That's why the employees of Transformer companies keep coming back, excitedly, to work. It's why they are loyal and engaged. Because it's just fun and exciting to do this work.

Given that over 70% of American employees report falling somewhere on the disengagement spectrum between neutrally bored and dramatically, toxically hateful about their company, it seems that the reengagement potential of a company-wide focus on serving the Transformational Consumer might be worth it, in and of itself.

Don't Just Talk about It, Be about It

I'll leave you with one last request: if you find the possibility of transcending the transactional relationship with your customers to be exciting or the potential remix of your company into a team of uber-productive, uber-engaged employees to be a worthy objective, do something about it.

Take it seriously.

The first step is thinking about the Transformational Consumer not as just a good buzzword to know but as a framework around which your teams can reorient, with time, resources and a well-designed set of objectives, process, and plan.

Treat it as a change-management challenge. Read up on what that means. Get some help and devote some real resources to creating an experience and a process of internal change to reorient your team or the company, to actually rethink what you sell, your customer, your marketing, your competition, and your culture.

The decks are stacked against you. Harvard Business School professor John Kotter writes that 70% of workplace change efforts fail. Flat out. I think they mostly fail because they are not resourced or conceived well from the beginning, as a process that can be optimized. There is a whole body of knowledge in the world about how to do this, how to do organizational change management successfully.

You're probably a Transformational Consumer, so do what Transformational Consumers do: read up on it! Hire a coach. Get professional help. (Call me.) Let this book be the first of many resources you tap as you explore how your company can transcend the transactional. Visit the Digital Dossier on TransformationalConsumer.com. Take a workshop or have us come to present to your team.

Read Kotter's original book *Leading Change* and his follow-up Harvard Business title, *Accelerate*.[3] Just like a Transformational Consumer would hire a personal trainer or a financial adviser, get some help from people who do this, helping companies change. Do what you would do in any other area of your life: research, learn, get help, put a plan in place. It is doable.

It is doable. Do not fall prey to the temptation to think that *your* business, your people, your customers, or your processes are uniquely impervious to change efforts and that it's really not possible so you'd be wise not to bother trying. Trust me when I say that (a) almost everyone thinks this, even businesses with just a couple of employees, and (b) change *can happen and does happen*. "This sweeping rethink of every part of our business will go super quickly, everyone will leap on board, and checks will be gleefully written to support it with no pushback," said no leader-hero ever.

The name of the game is to play it as it lays. Your company's rethink process doesn't have to look a certain way or look like another company's process. Your journey as leader-hero commences in earnest with creating a customized rethink strategy scoped and sequenced for the resources, priorities, past, present, and future of your particular organization and people.

My company is a research, management, and marketing consulting firm. But we actually have five core competences, which every single team member develops a skill set around, regardless of job role. Two of those five are organizational and individual behavior-change management.

We can't just deliver research projects, data indices, and beautiful customer journey maps to our client companies and not think about how to make them stick. That would defeat the entire purpose. Our company and project metrics are set around traditional business results, how successful our clients are at making these internal transformations and reorientations, *and* how successful our clients' Transformational Consumer reach and engagement initiatives are, in the final analysis.

For example, our goals include our own revenue, reach, engagement, and profitability metrics, but we also measure our success by answering the following questions for each project:

▲ Does our client company actually reach and engage Transformational Consumers, one, three and five years following our work together?

▲ Do our client company's brand love and engagement metrics actually take an uptick by virtue of the work we do together?

▲ Does our client company actually institutionalize the customer journey into its cultural events and experiences?

▲ Do teams all across the company actually begin using the Transformational Consumer framework, behavioral science, coaching/ change-management, or persuasive-design insights to drive some of their innovation, marketing, and internal communications practices?

When you approach the Transformational Consumer framework with objectives like this, it becomes crystal clear that it's not an overnight project to reorient in a way that serves these people and unlocks the engagement that has been limiting your business. But the results aren't fleeting, either. They can be lifelong: a lifelong, two-way love affair with your customer. That, I assure you, is worth the work.

Transcendence: The Natural State of Things

Now you are at the point in your Leader-Hero's Journey where it's time to embark on a voyage to that supernatural otherworld, beyond the world of business as usual and into the messy, human-centered realm of helping people change their lives.

Some things can't come with you on this path: cynicism, flippancy, learned helplessness, and fear, among them. These must be released, before you set out.

Then, you'll need to take stock and gear up for this journey.

You've got your guidebook. My team and I are available to you as a resource, even if only to point you in the right direction of others who can help. You might also need to bring on new sources of energy, tools, skills, practices, and helpers. Chances are good you're already getting a sense for what skills you'll need to bring on or cultivate in yourself or your team. At www.bkconnection.com/transformationalconsumer-sa, you'll find the Transformational Consumer Self-Assessment: What Do You Need to Rethink First? It'll help you get clearer about what your specific first step on the journey should be and help you sequence a custom roadmap for carrying out the rethinks in your own business.

If you want to go even deeper, at TransformationalConsumer.com you'll find a series of free resources to help you gear up, craft, and carry out your individual and organizational action plans for transcending the transactional. I highly recommend taking advantage of the following free resources at TransformationalConsumer.com, at the very least:

▲ The "Are you really a transformational leader?" individual self-assessment

▲ The Customer Loyalty and Engagement Audit

▲ The Customer Journey Mapping checklist.

This journey may be daunting, but it's also rewarding, professionally and personally. Guard against overwhelm by keeping one thing in mind. Transcending the transactional might seem like a fantastical, supernatural realm that you can only get to by winning a number of battles, internally and in the marketplace. This is true.

But carrying on a love affair with your customers is actually the most natural thing of all. To engage in relationships between customer and company on the basis of a mutually desired, mutually beneficial exchange of value for value is a return to the natural, original flow of commerce—this is the way things were before distrust and disengagement got in the way. When humans first began conducting commerce, it was not purely transactional: vendors played various societal roles, beyond selling stuff, and people had relationships with those who helped them stock their homes and make their lives function better than before. This is not new. This is a return to what's natural.

Workplaces in which people find opportunities for mastery, purpose, and engagement? This is not the norm now, but it is not supernatural. Rather, the current disengagement epidemic is super unnatural. The right and natural role of livelihood in our lives is to be a source of growth and expansion and joy and fulfillment. Creating a workplace conducive to engagement and transformation, inside and out, harks back to a time when people were so proud of our work that we made it part of our identity, taking the name Cooper, Smith, or Baker.

So, take heart, hero-leader. And then take the first step. That might be bringing this book to your next executive team meeting. It might be commissioning some research to get a better understanding of your own Transformational Consumer audience. It might be sitting down to do some informal online listening of your Transformational Consumer audience, right this moment. It could definitely be to write down, right now, the answer to this question: What is the human-scale, high-level problem our company exists to solve for our customers?

As is true for every personal disruption campaign and every HWW goal of the Transformational Consumer, the precise first step you take on your Leader-Hero's Journey is less important than that you take it. On that note, I'll close with a slightly different version of the 1951 W. H. Murray quote we looked at earlier, his notes in recounting a Scottish expedition he'd led into the Himalayas:

> But when I said that nothing had been done I erred in one important
> matter. We had definitely committed ourselves and were halfway out of
> our ruts. We had put down our passage money—booked a sailing to

Bombay. This may sound too simple, but is great in consequence. Until one is committed, there is hesitancy, the chance to draw back, always ineffectiveness. Concerning all acts of initiative (and creation), there is one elementary truth, the ignorance of which kills countless ideas and splendid plans: that the moment one definitely commits oneself, then Providence moves too.[1]

THE TRANSFORMATIONAL CONSUMER
SELF-ASSESSMENT

WHAT DO YOU NEED
TO RETHINK FIRST?

If you've made the decision to accept this call to adventure, it may seem as if you need to rethink everything in your entire business, fast. Once you're on fire and have a vision of transcendence, making wholesale, sweeping, cross-functional changes is tempting. It is also likely to be unsuccessful!

To get where you're going, you'll need a systematic, deliberate, and intentional action plan, roadmap, and change-management strategy. The leader-heroes who are successful in reorienting what they sell, their customers, marketing, competition, and teams are the ones who plan and execute their rethinks in a strategic manner, scoping, sequencing, and customizing them for their specific priorities, challenges, resources, and people.

The Transformational Consumer Self-Assessment: What Do You Need to Rethink First? is available from Berrett-Koehler Publishers at www.bkconnection.com/transformationalconsumer-sa. I designed this tool to give you an immediate way to begin sequencing your "rethink roadmap." The results will reveal the following:

▲ The highest impact changes and lowest investment power tweaks that your specific business should make to reach and engage Transformational Consumers

▲ The order of operations and priority that you should assign to the five rethinks

▲ The areas on which you should focus first if you have limited resources or challenges in the area of change management (e.g., you have a hard-to-change or entrenched team).

You can print out your results, which will include tips and action steps to take next. You may also take this self-assessment up to four times in

12 months. You might find it revealing and helpful to have all executive management team members take it, trade notes, and negotiate competing priorities before finalizing a change-management plan. To that end, bulk-order discounts are also available for organizational programs.

NOTES

Prologue

1. Deepak Chopra, *Quantum Healing: Exploring the Frontiers of Mind/Body Medicine* (New York: Bantam Books, 1989).

Introduction

1. Caitlin O'Connell, "23% of Users Abandon an App after One Use," *Localytics Blog*, May 26, 2013, http://info.localytics.com/blog/23-of-users-abandon-an-app -after-one-use.

2. Brian Monahan, "When It Comes to Ad Avoidance, the DVR Is Not the Problem," *AdAgeStat* (blog), May 24, 2011, http://adage.com/article/adagestat /smartphones-a-bigger-distraction-dvrs/227725/.

3. Amy Adkins, "Majority of U.S. Employees Not Engaged Despite Gains in 2014," Gallup, January 28, 2015, http://www.gallup.com/poll/181289/majority -employees-not-engaged-despite-gains-2014.aspx.

4. Michael Moss, *Salt, Sugar, Fat: How the Food Giants Hooked Us* (New York: Random House, 2014).

5. Michael Moss, "The Extraordinary Science of Addictive Junk Food," *New York Times*, February 20, 2013, http://www.nytimes.com/2013/02/24/magazine/the -extraordinary-science-of-junk-food.html?_r=0.

6. Ibid.

7. John Kell, "Soda Consumption Falls to 30-Year Low in the U.S.," *Fortune*, March, 29, 2016, http://fortune.com/2016/03/29/soda-sales-drop-11th-year/.

1. Meet the Transformational Consumer

1. I share much of the survey data in the pages that follow, as it provides such strong validation for the framework. The full survey report is available at TransformationalConsumer.com, at no cost if you own a copy of this book.

2. Individual transformational behaviors of a Transformational Consumer we'll call "efforts." The personal goals of an individual Transformational Consumer we'll refer to as "goals." A series of efforts to achieve a goal is a "campaign," and the lifelong stream of efforts, goals, and campaigns done in an effort to live healthier, wealthier, or wiser, we'll call "initiatives."

3. Carol Dweck, *Mindset: The New Psychology of Success* (New York: Ballantine Books, 2007).

4. Unilever, "Behaviour Change at Scale," accessed August 19, 2016, https://www .unilever.com/sustainable-living/the-sustainable-living-plan/improving-health-and -well-being/health-and-hygiene/changing-hygiene-habits-for-better-health /behaviour-change-at-scale.html.

5. Kira Wampler (Chief Marketing Officer, Lyft) and Joe Zadeh (Chief Product Officer, Airbnb), in discussion at South by Southwest media lunch moderated by the author, March 2015.

6. "Find Time for Your Goals with Google Calendar," *Official Google Blog*, April 28, 2016, https://googleblog.blogspot.com/2016/04/find-time-goals-google -calendar.html.

7. Tim Bradshaw, "Apple Boosts R&D Spending in New Product Hunt," *Financial Times*, October 28, 2014, http://www.ft.com/cms/s/0/f93b7122-5e57-11e4-bc04 -00144feabdc0.html#axzz4HnmLGDSd.

8. Lego, "The Method," accessed August 19, 2016, http://www.lego.com/en-us /seriousplay/the-method.

9. DisneyInstitute.com.

2. Removing Resistance and Triggering Progress

1. Eugene Wei, "Frictionless Product Design," *Remains of the Day* (blog), March 20, 2015, http://www.eugenewei.com/blog/2015/3/20/frictionless-product -design.

2. Spencer Lanoue, "IDEO's 6 Step Human-Centered Design Process: How to Make Things People Want," *User Testing* (blog), July 9, 2015, https://www.usertesting .com/blog/2015/07/09/how-ideo-uses-customer-insights-to-design-innovative -products-users-love/.

3. Timothy Ferriss, *The 4-Hour Chef: The Simple Path to Cooking Like a Pro, Learning Anything, and Living the Good Life* (Boston: New Harvest, 2012), 20.

4. Sigmund Freud, *The Standard Edition of the Complete Psychological Works of Sigmund Freud*, trans. and ed. James Strachey (London: Hogarth, 1994), 7:249–270, 20:75–175.

5. Steven Pressfield, *Do the Work: Overcome Resistance and Get Out of Your Own Way* (New York: Black Irish Entertainment, 2015), 7–9. Pressfield's other books are *The War of Art: Break through the Blocks and Win Your Creative Battles* (New York: Black Irish Entertainment, 2002) and, with Shawn Coyne, *Turning Pro: Tap Your Inner Power and Create Your Life's Work* (New York: Black Irish Entertainment, 2012).

6. Pressfield, *War of Art*, 6.

7. Jacquie Fuller, "How I Learned to Give Dieting the Middle Finger for Good," *Medium* (blog), July 1, 2016, https://medium.com/@jacquiefuller/how-i-learned-to -give-dieting-the-middle-finger-f10741b1116d#.r9t5iodo3.

8. "The 50/20/30 Rule for Minimalist Budgeting," *Mint Life* (blog), July 20, 2016, https://blog.mint.com/saving/the-minimalist-guide-to-budgeting-in-your-20s -072016/.

9. TrafficEstimate.com, accessed August 19, 2016.

10. "How Mint Grew to 1.5 Million Users and Sold for $170 Million in Just 2 Years," *Kissmetrics Blog*, accessed August 19, 2016, https://blog.kissmetrics.com /how-mint-grew/.

11. Anthony Wing Kosner, "Stanford's School of Persuasion: BJ Fogg on How to Win Users and Influence Behavior," *Forbes*, December 4, 2012, http://www.forbes .com/sites/anthonykosner/2012/12/04/stanfords-school-of-persuasion-bj-fogg-on -how-to-win-users-and-influence-behavior/#74d5d32d4c28.

12. B. J. Fogg, *Persuasive Technology: Using Computers to Change What We Think and Do* (San Francisco: Morgan Kaufmann, 2003), 24–26.

13. Ibid., 25.

14. Ibid.

15. Ibid., 25–26.

3. The Hero's Journey of Your Transformational Consumer

1. Joseph Campbell, *The Hero with a Thousand Faces* (Princeton: Princeton University Press, 1968), 30.

2. Christopher Booker, *The Seven Basic Plots: Why We Tell Stories* (London: Bloomsbury, 2004).

3. Martha Beck, *Finding Your Way in a Wild New World: Reclaim Your True Nature to Create the Life You Want* (New York: Atria Books, 2013).

4. David Richo, *How to Be an Adult in Relationships: The Five Keys to Mindful Loving* (Boston: Shambhala, 2002), 69.

5. Alex Williams, "The Paleo Lifestyle: The Way, Way Back," *New York Times*, September 19, 2014, http://www.nytimes.com/2014/09/21/fashion/the-paleo-lifestyle -the-way-way-way-back.html.

6. MyFitnessPal, *The Rise of the Fitness Tribe*, MyFitnessPal ebook, May 2014, http://blog-cdn1.myfitnesspal.com/wp-content/uploads/2014/05/MyFitnessTribe _Ebook_interactive_FINAL.pdf.

4. Your Call to Adventure

1. Josh Bersin, "Becoming Irresistible: A New Model for Employee Engagement," *Deloitte Review*, January 26, 2015, http://dupress.com/articles/employee-engagement -strategies/.

2. Brian Wansink and Jeffery Sobal, "Mindless Eating: The 200 Daily Food Decisions We Overlook," *Environment and Behavior* 39, no. 1 (2007): 106–123.

3. Michael Moss, "The Extraordinary Science of Addictive Junk Food," *New York Times*, February 20, 2013, http://www.nytimes.com/2013/02/24/magazine/the -extraordinary-science-of-junk-food.html.

4. Ibid.

5. Rethink What You Sell

1. Stuart Butterfield, "We Don't Sell Saddles Here," *Medium* (blog), February 17, 2014, https://medium.com/@stewart/we-dont-sell-saddles-here-4c59524d650d# .il03k2hnj.

2. Harry McCracken, "With 500,000 Users, Slack Says It's The Fastest-Growing Business App Ever," *Fast Company*, February 12, 2015, http://www.fastcompany.com /3042326/tech-forecast/with-500000-users-slack-says-its-the-fastest-growing -business-app-ever.

3. Tim Bradshaw, "Slack: Workplace Message App So Cute You Want to Use It at Home," *Financial Times*, March 26, 2015, http://www.ft.com/cms/s/0/bd7dbf46-d24c -11e4-9c25-00144feab7de.html.

4. Butterfield, "We Don't Sell Saddles Here."

5. Adam Grant, "The Surprising Habits of Original Thinkers," video, TED, February 2016, https://www.ted.com/talks/adam_grant_the_surprising_habits_of _original_thinkers/citations.

6. Butterfield, "We Don't Sell Saddles Here."

7. "Find Time for Your Goals with Google Calendar," *Official Google Blog*, April 28, 2016, https://googleblog.blogspot.com/2016/04/find-time-goals-google -calendar.html.

8. Christine Weil Schirmer (Head of Communications, Pinterest) in discussion with the author, March 28, 2016.

9. reddit.com/r/fitness.

10. Frances Cohen (Communications Manager, CreditKarma) in conversation with the author, April 29, 2016.

11. Jim Stengel, *Grow: How Ideals Power Growth and Profit at the World's Greatest Companies* (New York: Crown Business, 2011), 30, 36–41.

12. Ibid., 229.

13. Butterfield, "We Don't Sell Saddles Here."

14. Simon Sinek, *Start with Why: How Great Leaders Inspire Everyone to Take Action* (New York: Portfolio, 2011).

15. Sheryl Sandberg, *Lean In: Women, Work, and the Will to Lead* (New York: Knopf, 2013).

16. Arianna Huffington, *Thrive: The Third Metric to Redefining Success and Creating a Life of Well-Being, Wisdom, and Wonder* (New York: Harmony, 2015).

17. Mark Zuckerberg, "A Letter to Our Daughter," Facebook, December 1, 2015, https://www.facebook.com/notes/mark-zuckerberg/a-letter-to-our-daughter /10153375081581634/.

18. Alina Selukh, "Zuckerberg Tells Facebook Staff to Stop Crossing Out 'Black Lives Matter,'" NPR.org, February 26, 2016, http://www.npr.org/sections /alltechconsidered/2016/02/26/467985384/zuckerberg-tells-facebook-staff-to-stop -crossing-out-black-lives-matter.

19. Paul Ziobro, "Target Puts Some Food Suppliers on the Back Burner," *Wall Street Journal*, May 17, 2015, http://www.wsj.com/articles/target-puts-some-food -suppliers-on-the-back-burner-1431897130.

20. "Target Shares Roadmap to Transform Business, *A Bullseye View*" (blog), Target, March 3, 2015, https://corporate.target.com/press/releases/2015/03/target -shares-roadmap-to-transform-business.

21. Katie Thomas, Chad Bray, and Hiroko Tabuchi, "CVS to Buy 1,600 Drug-stores from Target for $1.9 Billion," *New York Times*, June 16, 2015, http://www .nytimes.com/2015/06/16/business/dealbook/cvs-agrees-to-buy-targets-pharmacy -business-for-1-9-billion.html.

22. Phil Wahba, "Target May Ditch Junk Food at the Counter," *Fortune*, September 16, 2015, http://fortune.com/2015/09/16/target-junk-food-health/.

23. Ibid.

24. "Get in Gear for the New Year: Target and SoulCycle Launch 10-City Tour," *A Bullseye View* (blog), Target, January 7, 2016, https://corporate.target.com/article /2016/01/soulcycle.

25. "Wellness for All: A Look at What's Next for Target's CSR Strategy," *A Bullseye View* (blog), Target, September 15, 2015, https://corporate.target.com/article /2015/09/csr-evolution.

6. Rethink Your Customer

1. "Four New Moments Every Marketer Should Know," *Think with Google*, June 2015, https://www.thinkwithgoogle.com/infographics/4-new-moments-every -marketer-should-know.html.

2. "An Intro to Micro-Moments: What We've Learned," video, *Think with Google*, accessed August 19, 2016, https://www.thinkwithgoogle.com/collections /micromoments.html.

3. "Micro-moments: Your Guide to Winning the Shift to Mobile," PDF report, *Think with Google*, accessed October 6, 2016, https://think.storage.googleapis.com /images/micromoments-guide-to-winning-shift-to-mobile-download.pdf.

4. Stuart Butterfield, "We Don't Sell Saddles Here," *Medium* (blog), February 17, 2014, https://medium.com/@stewart/we-dont-sell-saddles-here-4c59524d650d# .il03k2hnj.

5. Sarah Peterson, "Growing a Site from 0 to 10k Visitors a Month: Sarah Peterson Edition," *SumoMe* (blog), January 25, 2016, https://sumome.com/stories /first-10000-visitors-sarah-peterson.

6. Indi Young, *Mental Models: Aligning Design Strategy with Human Behavior* (Brooklyn, NY: Rosenfeld Media, 2008).

7. Warren Berger, *A More Beautiful Question: The Power of Inquiry to Spark Breakthrough Ideas* (New York: Bloomsbury, 2014).

8. Corn Refiners Association, "Sweeteners 360," available at, http://www .cornnaturally.com/sweetener-360.

7. Rethink Your Marketing

1. TrackMaven, "The Content Marketing Paradox," accessed August 19, 2016, http://trackmaven.com/resources/the-content-marketing-paradox-report/.

2. Brian Monahan, "When It Comes to Ad Avoidance, the DVR Is Not the Problem," *AdAgeStat* (blog), May 24, 2011, http://adage.com/article/adagestat /smartphones-a-bigger-distraction-dvrs/227725/.

3. Paul J. Zak, "Why Your Brain Loves Good Storytelling," *Harvard Business Review*, October 28, 2014, https://hbr.org/2014/10/why-your-brain-loves-good -storytelling.

4. Kevin Roberts, *Lovemarks: The Future beyond Brands*, 2nd ed. (Brooklyn, NY: powerHouse, 2005).

5. Ibid., 147.

6. Christine Weil Schirmer (Head of Communications, Pinterest) in discussion with the author, March 28, 2016.

7. Stephen Tobolowsky, *The Primary Instinct*, film, directed by David Chen (FilmBuff, 2015), Amazon Video.

8. James Patterson, "MasterClass on Writing," online course, MasterClass.com.

9. Steven Pressfield, *Nobody Wants to Read Your Sh*t: Why That Is and What You Can Do about It* (New York: Black Irish Entertainment, 2016).

10. Gunnar Lovelace (CEO, Thrive Market), interview with author, April 18, 2016.

8. Rethink Your Competition

1. Larry Menlo (President and CEO, CVS/health Corp.), "Message from Larry Merlo, President and CEO," video, *CVS Health* (blog), February 5, 2014, http://cvshealth.com/thought-leadership/expert-voices/message-from-larry-merlo-president-and-ceo.

2. Jeffrey Young, "Why Is CVS Walking Away from $2 Billion a Year?," *Huffington Post*, September 3, 2014, http://www.huffingtonpost.com/2014/09/03/cvs-cigarettes_n_5762212.html.

3. Jayne O'Donnell, "A Year Later, CVS Says Stopping Tobacco Sales Made a Big Difference," *USA Today*, September 25, 2015, http://www.usatoday.com/story/news/2015/09/02/cvs-stopping-tobacco-sales/71606590/.

4. CVS Health, *What Happens When You Start with Heart? CVS 2015 Annual Report*, accessed August 19, 2016, http://investors.cvshealth.com/~/media/Files/C/CVS-IR-v3/reports/2015-annual-report.pdf.

5. REI, "REI Overview," accessed August 19, 2016, https://www.rei.com/about-rei/business.html.

6. Tim Nudd, "REI Will Be Closed on Black Friday, and Pay Its 12,000 Employees Not to Work That Day," *AdWeek*, October 27, 2015, http://www.adweek.com/adfreak/rei-will-be-closed-black-friday-and-pay-its-12000-employees-not-work-day-167780.

7. Kevin Rose, "Foundation 20 // Elon Musk," video interview, YouTube, September 7, 2012, https://www.youtube.com/watch?v=L-s_3b5fRd8.

8. REI Staff, "Thank You for Choosing to #OptOutside with Us," *Co-Op Journal* (blog), accessed August 19, 2016, http://blog.rei.com/hike/thanks-for-choosing-to-optoutside-with-us/. Jeff Beer, "How Values and Purpose Made REI's #OptOutside a Big Winner at Cannes," FastCo Create, June 25, 2016, http://www.fastcocreate.com/3061312/cannes/how-values-and-purpose-made-reis-optoutside-a-big-winner-at-cannes.

9. Lee Chae (Head of Bioinformatics, Hampton Creek), private conversation with the author, February 23, 2016.

10. Stephanie Strom, "After Suing over Eggless Spread, Hellman's Introduces Its Own," *New York Times*, February 2, 2016, http://www.nytimes.com/2016/02/03/business/after-suing-over-eggless-spread-hellmanns-introduces-its-own.html?_r=0.

9. Rethink Your Culture

1. Timothy Ferriss, *The 4-Hour Workweek: Escape 9–5, Live Anywhere, and Join the New Rich* (New York: Harmony, 2009); Chris Guillebeau, *The $100 Startup:*

Reinvent the Way You Make a Living, Do What You Love, and Create a New Future (New York: Crown Business, 2012).

2. Henry Cloud, *Integrity: The Courage to Meet the Demands of Reality* (New York: Harper Business, 2009).

3. John Kotter, *Leading Change* (Cambridge, MA: Harvard Business Review Press, 2012); John Kotter, *Accelerate: Building Strategic Agility for a Faster-Moving World* (Cambridge, MA: Harvard Business Review Press, 2014).

Conclusion

1. William H. Murray, *The Scottish Himalayan Expedition* (London: Dent, 1951).

ACKNOWLEDGMENTS

I thank my Heavenly Father for His grace, mercy, and favor; for the life I've been blessed to live and the work I've been blessed to do; and for the flow of concepts and words that became this book.

I thank my earthly parents and my grandmother for their love, for my life, and for their limitless belief and investment in what I could do and be in this world, from literally day one.

I thank the entrepreneurs, executives, marketers, and Transformational Consumers I've had the privilege of working with over the years. In particular, to Mike and Al Lee and every member of the MyFitnessPal executive management team (Karthik, Vijay, Randall, Marybeth, Warren): it was a privilege to build such a beautiful, impactful organization with you. I look forward to getting the band back together, one of these days.

I thank the members of my teams at TCI, MyFitnessPal/UACF, and Re-think Multimedia, in particular: Jennifer Jostedt Lauricella (who pressed pause on the whole wide world for me so I could go into monk mode and write this book), Brandi Luedeman, Elle Penner, Barbara Seif, Demi Tsasis, Sabrina Tillman Grotewold, Trinh Le, Sarah Morgan, Tierra Wilson, and Christian Clough. I've said that my team-building strategy is one genius (me) and 100 geniuses (my team), and you definitely prove that out. Thank you for spending these seasons of your career with me. Squad goals: achieved.

I thank my same brain, Rebecca Silliman, for things too massive and too numerous to bother trying to express with words.

I thank my writing coach, Linden Gross, for activating and developing me as a writer. And I offer my deep gratitude and love to my past/present/future literary agent, Lisa Gallagher, for so much wise counsel over the years and for being my adviser and my friend.

And certainly not least, I thank the team at Berrett-Koehler Publishers, Steve Piersanti, Jeevan Sivasubramaniam, Charlotte Ashlock, Kristen Frantz, and Shabnam Banerjee-McFarland, for bringing this book to life and for modeling what a company that unapologetically commits itself to serving Transformational Consumers (and also humanity) can look like, in an ideal case. They have been engaged, thoughtful collaborators and conscious champions of this work since they first heard about it. I am humbled and grateful for their partnership in building this movement.

INDEX

ABOUT THE AUTHOR

Tara-Nicholle Nelson is the founder and CEO of Transformational Consumer Insights (TCI) a customer research and strategy firm. TCI creates marketing, content, product, and positioning strategies based on deep human insights. The company's sweet spot is helping startups and established companies spot opportunities for innovation, drive customer loyalty, and build beloved brands by reaching and engaging Transformational Consumers. Nelson speaks and writes about transformation, leadership, and marketing, and coaches a small group of entrepreneurs and executives through transitions and their own personal hero's journeys.

Tara-Nicholle Nelson

Nelson was the vice president of marketing for MyFitnessPal, now part of Under Armour. In her first year on the job, MyFitnessPal grew from 45 million to more than 100 million users, her team drove a 22% increase in user engagement, and the company went from raising an $18 million Series A investment round to being acquired by Under Armour for $475 million.

Nelson's teams covered growth, engagement, communications, media relations, content marketing, social media, and user-insights programs across the digital health and fitness brands MyFitnessPal, MapMyFitness, Endomondo, and UnderArmour.com.

Previously, Nelson was the CEO of Rethink Multimedia and, before that, the VP of digital and content at the SutherlandGold Group. At these agencies, she created and led execution of content, PR, and executive thought leadership strategies for companies including MyFitnessPal, Eventbrite, Trulia, Lookout Mobile Security, and Chegg. Her career began as a real estate attorney and broker and then took a turn into tech as a content-marketing strategist and spokesperson for such companies as HGTV and Trulia.

Nelson holds a master's degree in psychology and a Juris Doctorate from the University of California, Berkeley. Tara is the board president of City Slicker Farms, a nonprofit food-justice organization in West Oakland. She considers herself a world-class brunch athlete and is the devoted servant of the pug dogs Aiko and Sumiko.

Berrett–Koehler
Publishers

Berrett-Koehler is an independent publisher dedicated to an ambitious mission: *Connecting people and ideas to create a world that works for all.*

We believe that the solutions to the world's problems will come from all of us, working at all levels: in our organizations, in our society, and in our own lives. Our BK Business books help people make their organizations more humane, democratic, diverse, and effective (we don't think there's any contradiction there). Our BK Currents books offer pathways to creating a more just, equitable, and sustainable society. Our BK Life books help people create positive change in their lives and align their personal practices with their aspirations for a better world.

All of our books are designed to bring people seeking positive change together around the ideas that empower them to see and shape the world in a new way.

And we strive to practice what we preach. At the core of our approach is Stewardship, a deep sense of responsibility to administer the company for the benefit of all of our stakeholder groups including authors, customers, employees, investors, service providers, and the communities and environment around us. Everything we do is built around this and our other key values of quality, partnership, inclusion, and sustainability.

This is why we are both a B-Corporation and a California Benefit Corporation—a certification and a for-profit legal status that require us to adhere to the highest standards for corporate, social, and environmental performance.

We are grateful to our readers, authors, and other friends of the company who consider themselves to be part of the BK Community. We hope that you, too, will join us in our mission.

A BK Business Book

We hope you enjoy this BK Business book. BK Business books pioneer new leadership and management practices and socially responsible approaches to business. They are designed to provide you with groundbreaking and practical tools to transform your work and organizations while upholding the triple bottom line of people, planet, and profits. High-five!

To find out more, visit **www.bkconnection.com**.

Berrett–Koehler
Publishers

Connecting people and ideas
to create a world that works for all

Dear Reader,

Thank you for picking up this book and joining our worldwide community of Berrett-Koehler readers. We share ideas that bring positive change into people's lives, organizations, and society.

To welcome you, we'd like to offer you a free e-book. You can pick from among twelve of our bestselling books by entering the promotional code **BKP92E** here: http://www.bkconnection.com/welcome.

When you claim your free e-book, we'll also send you a copy of our e-newsletter, the *BK Communiqué*. Although you're free to unsubscribe, there are many benefits to sticking around. In every issue of our newsletter you'll find

- A free e-book
- Tips from famous authors
- Discounts on spotlight titles
- Hilarious insider publishing news
- A chance to win a prize for answering a riddle

Best of all, our readers tell us, "Your newsletter is the only one I actually read." So claim your gift today, and please stay in touch!

Sincerely,

Charlotte Ashlock
Steward of the BK Website

Questions? Comments? Contact me at bkcommunity@bkpub.com.

Certified

Corporation
bcorporation.net